FOREIGN LANGUAGE COURSES

Power-Glide
Children's Spanish Level III

Activity Book

by

Robert W. Blair

This product would not have been possible without the assistance of many people. The help of those mentioned below was invaluable.

Editorial, Design and Production Staff

Instructional Design: Robert Blair, Ph.D.

Project Coordinator: James Blair

Development Manager: David Higginbotham

Story Writer: Natalie Prado

Cover Design: Guy Francis

Contributing Editors: Gretchen Hilton, Emily Spackman, Phillip Morris

Audio Voices: Dell Blair, Luke Drake, Robert Blair, Rebeca Witham, Jaime Reyna, R. Seth Bird, Karina Herbert,

Illustrator: Apryl Robertson

Translators: Phillip Morris, Robert Blair

Musicians: Geoff Groberg, Rob Fulkerson

Audio Recording, Editing and Mixing: Rob Fulkerson

Power-Glide Foreign Language Courses
1682 W 820 N, Provo, UT 84601
(8/01)

Contents

A Note to Parents

Basic Course Objectives

The major goal of this course is to keep children excited about communicating in another language. The adventure story, the variety of activities, and the simplified teaching methods employed in the course are all designed to make learning interesting and fun.

This course is primarily for children 2nd through 4th grade. Course activities are designed specifically with these learners in mind and include matching games, story telling, speaking, drawing, creative and deductive thinking, acting, and guessing—all things which children do for fun!

Ultimately, children who complete the course can expect to understand an impressive amount of Spanish, including common Spanish phrases, complete Spanish sentences, Spanish numbers, rhymes, and questions. They will also be able to understand stories told all or mostly in Spanish, to retell these stories themselves using Spanish, and to make up stories of their own using words and sentence patterns they have learned.

Children who complete the course will be well prepared to continue learning with our other Spanish courses, and they will have the foundation that will make learning at that level just as fun and interesting, albeit more challenging, as in this course.

Teaching Techniques

This course allows your children to learn by doing, to learn through enjoyable experiences. The idea is to put the experience first and the explanation after. This is important to note because it is directly opposite to how teaching—and especially foreign language teaching—is traditionally done. Typically foreign language teachers spend the majority of their time explaining complex grammar and syntax rules, and drilling students on vocabulary. In this traditional mode, rules and lists come first and experience comes last. Learning experientially, on the other hand, simulates the natural language acquisition process of children.

When children learn their native languages apparently effortlessly in early childhood, it is not through the study of grammar rules and vocabulary lists. Rather, they learn the words for things around them simply by listening to others, and they intuitively grasp an amazing amount of grammar and syntax in the same way. By using activities that simulate natural language acquisition, it is not only possible but normal for children to learn a new language quickly and enjoy doing it!

Specifically, this course motivates your children to learn Spanish by providing learning experiences in the form of matching games, story telling exercises, drawing exercises, singing and acting, and other fun activities aimed at developing functional language comprehension and speaking ability. These activities contrast markedly with the exercises in more traditional courses, which tend to focus exclusively on learning some vocabulary, or on understanding very simple Spanish sentences, without extending learning to the point of actually understanding and speaking the language. The language your children will acquire through this course will be more useful to them than language learned through traditional approaches, because knowledge gained in fun, rather than stressful, ways is much easier for children to retain and much more natural for them to use themselves.

Using the Course

This course is carefully designed so that it can be used either by children working primarily on their own or by parents and children working closely together. Complete instructions, simple enough to be easily followed by children, are included on the audios. Parents or other adults can enhance the course significantly by acting as facilitators: reviewing instructions, encouraging creativity and course participation, providing frequent opportunities for children to display what they have learned, rewarding effort and accomplishment, and providing enthusiasm. Keep in mind that much of the real learning takes place as you interact with your children during and after the course learning experiences.

Perhaps the most important of the above ways parents can help their children is to give them an audience for their new skills. In order to facilitate this invaluable help, we have added a new feature to the Children's Level III Spanish Course. At the end of each activity or story we have included suggestions for a Performance Challenge. One goal of Power-Glide courses is to teach students to produce the target language creatively and independently. The new Performance Challenge feature will help children do just that. These additional exercises will increase your child's fluency, pronunciation, and confidence in the target language, as well as give you the opportunity to be directly involved in the learning process. Encourage your children to use as much Spanish as possible and give them the audience they need to perform for. Remind your students not to worry about mistakes. Rather, encourage them to review any words they may struggle with and make sure they feel comfortable with the current material before moving to the next lesson.

Using the resources provided in the course book and on the audios, an adult learning facilitator does not need to know Spanish or how to teach it in order to be a great learning partner. In fact, one of the most enjoyable and effective ways to learn is together, as a team.

Parents or other adults who know Spanish can, of course, supplement the materials in this course very effectively. A proficient bilingual teacher could, for example: (1) help children learn additional vocabulary by putting several objects on table and asking and answering questions about them, such as "What is this?" or "Where is the _____?", and so on; (2) create on-the-spot diglot-weave stories by reading illustrated children's books such as Silverstein's *Are You My Mother?*, putting key words (picturable nouns) into Spanish, and asking questions about the story or its pictures partly or completely in Spanish; (3) involve children in making and doing things (such as making a paper airplane or finding a hidden object) giving instructions all or partly in Spanish.

We have added another new feature to this course that will make it easier to use. For each audio track, you will see a CD icon that includes the CD number and the track number. This will help you to easily find your place from lesson to lesson.

Benefits of Second Language Acquisition

Learning a second language has many benefits. Besides the obvious value of being able to understand and communicate with others, research in the United States and Canada in the 1970s and '80s has shown that learning a second language gives children a distinct advantage in general school subject areas. Seeing linguistic and cultural contrasts as they acquire a second language, children gain insight not only into the new language and cultures, but into their own language and culture as well.

Furthermore, a considerable amount of research has shown that learning a second language in childhood helps children learn to read and write their native language. Quite possibly the best phonics training a child can receive is to learn a language like Spanish, because Spanish spelling is quite phonetic: when one knows Spanish, the spelling of a Spanish word tells him or her how to pronounce it, and (with few exceptions) the sound of a Spanish word tells him or her how to spell it. This carries over to English and helps children intuitively understand how language works.

Our Goal

Our goal at Power-Glide is to change the way the U.S. studies language. We want to produce foreign language speakers, not just studiers. This Children's Level III Spanish Course effectively continues the road to speaking Spanish. We hope you and your children will find delight in the ongoing adventure of learning another language.

7 The Adventure Continues

The Adventure Continues

(Yucatán)

 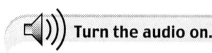 **Turn the audio on.**

Track 1

Narrator: You stand on the shore of Playa Lancheros, a beach on the south side of Isla Mujeres. You can't believe all of the adventures that have led up to this moment! When you came down to Yucatán to visit your grandpa Glen last week, you ended up having to solve clues and learn a lot of Spanish to find him. Now your grandpa is so impressed with how much you have learned that he has agreed to take you out with him to search for the treasure stolen by the pirate, Don Diego de Consuelo. Don Diego's memoirs indicated that the next puzzle-clue would be hidden somewhere on Playa Lancheros.

Grandpa Glen: Okay, Tony, Lisa, we've got a lot of searching to do. The clue in the memoirs is "En el diente del tigre." Do you know what that means?

Tony: "Tigre" means tiger, I remember that.

Grandpa: Good. "Diente" means tooth, so "en el diente del tigre" means "in the tiger's tooth." Okay? Let's go and look.

Lisa: This is great! Can we go swimming?

Grandpa: Actually, Lisa, this part of the beach is restricted to swimmers. They use this area to protect sea turtles.

Tony: Sea turtles. Aren't they endangered?

Grandpa: Yes, they are. It's a good thing for them that the beach is closed, and for us too, because it'll be a lot less crowded. Just be careful, and stay away from the pens they've set up for the turtles.

Narrator: You both promise and begin to search the beach. The sun is out, and the white sand is nearly blinding.

Lisa: I don't know how we're going to find any tigers on the beach. Shouldn't we look somewhere else?

Tony: No . . . look, over there at that rock! It looks kind of like a tiger's head.

Lisa: You're right. It does. Cool! Let's go and look.

Narrator: You both run over to the rock and look at it.

Tony: Wow. That's kind of scary. It looks real. I don't want to have to reach in the mouth.

Lisa: Come on. I want to see.

Narrator: You reach in the mouth of the tiger and feel around. After a moment you find a piece of parchment. You pull it out.

Tony: We found it! We're going to find that treasure in no time!

Lisa: Great! Let's go and show Grandpa Glen.

Narrator: Your grandpa is very impressed with how quickly you found the puzzle-clue. You all look it over together.

Grandpa Glen: Look, children. It says, "Vaya a donde Juan Paco Pedro come los viernes."

Tony: That sounds hard.

Grandpa: Yes. I won't be sure what it means until I check the pirate's memoirs back at the hotel.

 Turn the audio off.

Broken Window, Three Pigs, Farmer & Turnip

(Diglot Weave Review)

 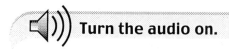 **Turn the audio on.**

Track 2

Narrator: You're heading back to the hotel in Cancún, where you have been staying, to check Don Diego's memoirs.

Lisa: I can't wait. This is so exciting.

Grandpa: Yes, it is, Lisa, but don't forget why I've invited you and Tony to come along. I want you to learn as much from this adventure as you can.

Tony: But, Grandpa, we have been learning!

Grandpa: You remember all you've learned on this adventure, and what I taught you back at home?

Lisa: Of course we do!

Grandpa: Well, I'd like you to show me. After all, I need to be able to count on you. Tell me the story about the "ventana rota."

Tony: Okay . . . um . . . I can't remember it all.

Grandpa: All right, I know that was a long time ago. Let me go over some of the stories with you again, and make sure you remember them this time!

Track 3

You remember the cuento I told you about some niños playing en la calle in front of una casa. You remember that uno of the niños tiró una pelota, y la pelota crashed through una ventana y hit un hombre who was reading a libro. La pelota le pegó right in la nariz. And you remember that el hombre was angry . . . muy enojado. El hombre gritó to los niños, "Stop! Wait!" But los niños started running up la calle. But when they saw una mujer walking down la calle toward them, they turned off y ran into el bosque where a feroz lobo was hiding behind un árbol, only la cola del lobo showing from behind el árbol. And you remember that un perro chased el feroz lobo and bit him on la cola, pero el lobo got away. And then los niños went back to la casa y knocked on la puerta, y el hombre came to la puerta. But he wasn't mean; he didn't scold . . . no regañó as they expected him to do. El hombre habló kindly to them, and this is what he dijo: "I'm just glad you weren't eaten by el lobo. I'm just glad that el perro chased away el lobo, y you're still alive.

Now, well there's more to the cuento. You see, that big perro that chased off el feroz lobo, it belongs to a mujer, la mujer that was walking down la calle when el niño tiró la pelota y la pelota crashed through la ventana y le pegó al hombre right en la nariz. El hombre invited los niños into his casa and they were talking there when there came another golpe a la puerta. El hombre opened la puerta y standing there was la mujer y el big perro wagging his cola. El hombre invited a la mujer y su perro to come in y sentarse. Then la mujer dijo, "Mi perro and I live en una casa en el bosque. Y mi perro y yo like to take walks en el bosque. A few months ago we were walking en el bosque and came upon tres cochinitos. We hid behind un árbol y listened to their conversation. It was a conversación about building una casa.

Uno de los cochinitos dijo to his older hermanos, 'I want to . . .Yo quiero hacerme una casa de paja. What do you think, hermanos?'

El segundo cochinito dijo, 'If you want, you can ... tú puedes hacerte una casa de paja, but I won't help you . . . No, sir, hermanito, yo no te ayudo. Yo no quiero to live en una casa de paja.'

'¿Por qué no?' asked the younger brother.

'It's dangerous . . . Es muy peligroso.'

'¿Peligroso?'

'Sí, muy peligroso.'

'¿Cómo?'

'Una casa de paja is so light . . . tan ligera that it would be very easy for el big, bad lobo to soplar y foplar y tumbar it.'

'I agree . . . Estoy de acuerdo,' dijo the first pig, el hermano mayor. 'Don't be foolish and build una casa de paja.' Pero el cochinito no listened to the wise counsel of his hermanos. He went y se hizo una casa de paja.

Then el segundo cochinito dijo, 'Yo quiero hacerme una casa de leñas. ¿Qué piensas tú, hermano?' he asked su hermano mayor.

'If you want, you can . . . tú puedes hacerte una casa de leñas, but I won't help you . . . No, sir, hermanito, yo no te ayudo. Yo no quiero to live en una casa de leñas.'

'¿Por qué no?' asked el segundo cochinito.

'¡Porque es muy peligroso!'

'¿Peligroso?'

'Sí, muy peligroso.'

'¿Cómo?'

'Una casa de leñas. is so light . . . tan ligera . . . that it would be easy . . . muy fácil . . . for el big, bad lobo to soplar y foplar y tumbarla.' Pero el segundo cochinito no listened to the wise counsel of his hermano mayor. He went y se hizo una casa de leñas.

El hermano mayor dijo, 'Yo quiero hacerme una casa de ladrillos. Pues, una casa de ladrillos es firme. El lobo no puede tumbarla.' So, el cochinito mayor wisely se hizo una casa de ladrillos, una casa muy firme."

You know the rest of the cuento, and how it ends when el lobo finally gives up y sale, unable to tumbar la casa de ladrillos. But you may not have heard qué pasó after that. As he was running along home, he heard this sonido: "Unh! Mmm! Ugh!" He stopped and hid behind un árbol. From there he watched something he had never seen before. Here is what el lobo vio: había un hombre, a farmer, holding on to una planta, y una mujer agarrando al hombre, y un perro agarrando a la mujer, y un gato agarrando al perro. They were trying to pull up a giant nabo, but try as they might, they could not get el nabo out.

Just then un ratoncito came up al lobo y dijo, "Eh, Señor Lobo, mire, they need help . . . ellos necesitan ayuda. Come on . . . vamos. Vamos a ayudarles."

"No," dijo el lobo. "Not me . . . Yo no. You can go and try to ayudarlos. Me, I'll just wait here and watch to see qué pasa."

Well, you know the rest of that cuento, but did you know that after that, el lobo started to pensar, "Wow! that little ratoncito had the right attitude. Without his ayuda they could not have gotten el nabo out. Maybe if I had a better attitude, if I weren't so selfish, maybe if I were willing to ayudar a otros more, people would start to like me, and I would be happier."

Y believe it or not . . . créalo o no from that time on, el lobo began to change. He decided that he would no longer soplar y foplar y try to tumbar casas. No longer would he threaten los niños en el bosque. He would find a way to be a friend . . . un amigo to someone, rather than un enemigo to everyone..

 Turn the audio off.

Days of the Week

(Ditties)

 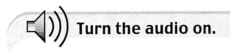 **Turn the audio on.**

Track 4

Narrator: You all arrive at the hotel room in Cancún.

Grandpa: Wait. There's something wrong here.

Lisa: What is it?

Grandpa: The door is open. I closed it when we left.

Narrator: Frightened, you follow your grandpa into the room. All of your things have been scattered around, and chairs knocked over.

Tony: We've been robbed! This is terrible.

Grandpa: Yes, it is. Look, they found where I hid Don Diego's memoirs.

Lisa: Oh, no! We'll never find the treasure without the memoirs!

Tony: Wait! I bet I know who broke in. It must have been Malo! I know he still wants the treasure. Remember when he followed us down into the Cenote Zaci, Lisa, and we were so scared?

Lisa: Yes, of course. It must have been him! He's trying to find the treasure!

Grandpa: Well, if that's true, then we'll have to find the treasure without the memoirs. We can't let it fall into Malo's hands.

Tony: Do you think we'll be able to find it?

Grandpa: Well, I still have all my folklore research, and I remember some things that I read from the memoirs . . . yes, I think we can still do it. We'll have to work fast, though, because Malo will have the advantage. Not only does he have the memoirs, he is a native Spanish speaker. You'll have to start learning faster than ever if we're going to keep up with him.

Lisa: Right!

Narrator: You help Grandpa Glen search through his folklore papers, looking for something that will relate to the clue, "Vaya a donde Juan Paco Pedro come los viernes."

Tony: Grandpa, look. This has the word "viernes" in it.

Grandpa: Let me see . . . oh yes! Of course! This song is about the days of the week, and lists things to eat on each day. Do you think you can learn it?

Lisa: Of course!

Grandpa: Okay. This song is common in Mexico and Central America. It lists all the days of the week and gives a specific food eaten on that day. Pay attention for "viernes," Friday, because that's the day we're looking for. Let's start with Monday, "lunes."

Hoy es lunes, hoy es lunes,   *(Today is Monday, today is Monday,)*

Lunes: queso,   (*Monday: cheese,*)

Todos tienen hambre.   (*Everybody is hungry.*)

Vamos a comer!   (*Let's eat!*)

Here's Tuesday, "martes," in which we eat "plátano." Then we repeat what we've eaten so far this week.

Hoy es martes, hoy es martes,   (*Today is Tuesday, today is Tuesday,*)

Martes: plátano, lunes: queso,   (*Tuesday: banana, Monday: cheese,*)

Todos tienen hambre,   (*Everybody is hungry.*)

Vamos a comer!   (*Let's eat!*)

Then we do "miércoles":

Hoy es miércoles, hoy es miércoles,   (*Today is Wednesday, today is Wednesday,*)

Miércoles: mole, martes: plátano, lunes: queso,   (*Wednesday: mole, Tuesday: banana, Monday: cheese*)

Todos tienen hambre,   (*Everybody is hungry.*)

Vamos a comer!   (*Let's eat!*)

And:

Hoy es jueves, hoy es jueves,   (*Today is Thursday, today is Thursday,*)

Jueves: rosbif, miércoles: mole, martes: plátano, lunes: queso,   (*Thursday: roast beef, Wednesday: mole, Tuesday: banana, Monday: cheese.*)

Todos tienen hambre,   (*Everybody is hungry.*)

Vamos a comer!   (*Let's eat!*)

Hoy es viernes, hoy es viernes,   (*Today is Friday, today is Friday,*)

Viernes: chile, jueves: rosbif, miércoles: mole, martes: plátano, lunes: queso,   (*Friday: chile, Thursday: roast beef, Wednesday: mole, Tuesday: banana, Monday: cheese.*)

Todos tienen hambre,   (*Everybody is hungry.*)

Vamos a comer!   (*Let's eat!*)

Hoy es sábado, hoy es sábado,   (*Today is Saturday, today is Saturday,*)

Sábado: pinole, viernes: chile, jueves: rosbif, miércoles: mole, martes: plátano, lunes: queso,

(Saturday: pinole, Friday: chile, Thursday: roast beef, Wednesday: mole, Tuesday: banana, Monday:cheese.)

Todos tienen hambre,

(Everybody is hungry.)

Vamos a comer!

(Let's eat!)

Hoy es domingo, hoy es domingo,

(Today is Sunday, today is Sunday,)

Domingo: frijoles, sábado: pinole, viernes: chile, jueves: rosbif, miércoles: mole, martes: plátano, lunes: queso,

(Sunday: beans, Saturday: pinole, Friday: chile, Thursday: roast beef, Wednesday: mole, Tuesday: banana, Monday:cheese.)

Todos tienen hambre,

(Everybody is hungry.)

Vamos a comer!

(Let's eat!)

And that's the whole week. Do you think you can sing it with me?

Lisa: Sure!

Grandpa: Okay, here we go, starting at "lunes."

Grandpa, Tony & Lisa:

Hoy es lunes, hoy es lunes,

(Today is Monday, today is Monday,)

Lunes: queso,

(Monday: cheese,)

Todos tienen hambre.

(Everybody is hungry.)

Vamos a comer!

(Let's eat!)

Hoy es martes, hoy es martes,

(Today is Tuesday, today is Tuesday,)

Martes: plátano, lunes queso,

(Tuesday: banana, Monday: cheese,)

Todos tienen hambre,

(Everybody is hungry.)

Vamos a comer!

(Let's eat!)

Hoy es miércoles, hoy es miércoles,

(Today is Wednesday, today is Wednesday,)

Miércoles: mole, martes, plátano, lunes queso,

(Wednesday: mole, Tuesday: banana, Monday: cheese)

Todos tienen hambre,

(Everybody is hungry.)

Vamos a comer!

(Let's eat!)

Hoy es jueves, hoy es jueves,	*(Today is Thursday, today is Thursday,)*
Jueves: rosbif, miércoles, mole, martes, plátano, lunes queso,	*(Thursday: roast beef, Wednesday: mole Tuesday: banana, Monday: cheese.)*
Todos tienen hambre,	*(Everybody is hungry.)*
Vamos a comer!	*(Let's eat!)*
Hoy es viernes, hoy es viernes,	*(Today is Friday, today is Friday,)*
Viernes: chile, jueves, rosbif, miércoles, mole, martes, plátano, lunes queso,	*(Friday: chile, Thursday: roast beef, Wednesday: mole, Tuesday: banana, Monday: cheese.)*
Todos tienen hambre,	*(Everybody is hungry.)*
Vamos a comer!	*(Let's eat!)*
Hoy es sábado, hoy es sábado,	*(Today is Saturday, today is Saturday,)*
Sábado: pinole, viernes, chile, jueves, rosbif, miércoles, mole, martes, plátano, lunes queso,	*(Saturday: pinole, Friday: chile, Thursday: roast beef, Wednesday: mole, Tuesday: banana, Monday:cheese.)*
Todos tienen hambre,	*(Everybody is hungry.)*
Vamos a comer!	*(Let's eat!)*
Hoy es domingo, hoy es domingo,	*(Today is Sunday, today is Sunday,)*
Domingo: frijoles, sábado, pinole, viernes, chile, jueves, rosbif, miércoles, mole, martes, plátano, lunes queso,	*(Sunday: beans, Saturday: pinole, Friday: chile, Thursday: roast beef, Wednesday: mole, Tuesday: banana, Monday:cheese.)*
Todos tienen hambre,	*(Everybody is hungry.)*
Vamos a comer!	*(Let's eat!)*

Grandpa: Great!

 Turn the audio off.

Performance Challenge:

Now that you have learned a new song, share your Spanish with a parent, friend, or one of your brothers and sisters by teaching them the song. Remember to teach it in Spanish and then translate the words into English if your partner does not understand Spanish. For an even greater challenge, try writing a song about your culture and put it to the tune of the Spanish song you just learned. If you need an idea to get you started, just think of what a visitor from another country would like to know about you and your family.

Juan Paco Pedro de la Mar

(Ditties)

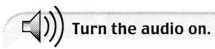 **Turn the audio on.**

Track 5 **Grandpa:** Okay. So, what do we eat on "viernes"?

Lisa: Um, "chile," right?

Grandpa: Right. That part of the clue means "chile."

Tony: But wait! There's a second part to the clue. Remember? The part with Juan Paco . . . what was it?

Grandpa: Juan Paco Pedro. I think I know the song that answers that. . .let me see. Here it is. This is a fun song. It is about a man with a very long name. Listen. The first time you sing it loudly.

Juan Paco Pedro de la Mar,	*(Juan Paco Pedro de le Mar,)*
Es mi nombre, sí.	*(Is my name, yes.)*
Y cuando yo me voy,	*(And when I go out,)*
Me dicen que yo soy,	*(They tell me that I am,)*
Juan Paco Pedro de la Mar.	*(Juan Paco Pedro de le Mar,)*
La la la la la la la . . .	*(La la la la la la la . . .)*

Okay, now you sing it a second time, except you are quieter on the verse, and the la la's are still loud. Like this.

Juan Paco Pedro de la Mar,	*(Juan Paco Pedro de le Mar,)*
Es mi nombre, sí.	*(Is my name, yes.)*
Y cuando yo me voy,	*(And when I go out,)*
Me dicen que yo soy,	*(They tell me that I am,)*
Juan Paco Pedro de la Mar.	*(Juan Paco Pedro de le Mar,)*
La la la la la la la . . .	*(La la la la la la la . . .)*

Now, the last time. You whisper the first part as softly as you can, then still yell out the end. Okay?

Juan Paco Pedro de la Mar,	*(Juan Paco Pedro de le Mar,)*
Es mi nombre, sí.	*(Is my name, yes.)*
Y cuando yo me voy,	*(And when I go out,)*
Me dicen que yo soy,	*(They tell me that I am,)*
Juan Paco Pedro de la Mar.	*(Juan Paco Pedro de le Mar,)*

La la la la la la la!   (*La la la la la la la . . .*)

Do you think that you can sing that with me?

Grandpa, Tony & Lisa:

Juan Paco Pedro de la Mar,   (*Juan Paco Pedro de le Mar,*)

Es mi nombre, sí.   (*Is my name, yes.*)

Y cuando yo me voy,   (*And when I go out,*)

Me dicen que yo soy,   (*They tell me that I am,*)

Juan Paco Pedro de la Mar.   (*Juan Paco Pedro de le Mar,*)

La la la la la la la . . .   (*La la la la la la la . . .*)

Juan Paco Pedro de la Mar,   (*Juan Paco Pedro de le Mar,*)

Es mi nombre, sí.   (*Is my name, yes.*)

Y cuando yo me voy,   (*And when I go out,*)

Me dicen que yo soy,   (*They tell me that I am,*)

Juan Paco Pedro de la Mar.   (*Juan Paco Pedro de le Mar,*)

La la la la la la la . . .   (*La la la la la la la . . .*)

Juan Paco Pedro de la Mar,   (*Juan Paco Pedro de le Mar,*)

Es mi nombre, sí.   (*Is my name, yes.*)

Y cuando yo me voy,   (*And when I go out,*)

Me dicen que yo soy,   (*They tell me that I am,*)

Juan Paco Pedro de la Mar.   (*Juan Paco Pedro de le Mar,*)

La la la la la la la!   (*La la la la la la la . . .*)

Grandpa: Great! You're picking this up fast.

 Turn the audio off.

Performance Challenge:

The first clue to finding the treasure talks about what Juan Paco Pedro eats. You have already tried a few recipes that are authentic to Hispanic culture. In the back of your Activity Book, you'll find even more great recipes. In order to get into the spirit of this adventure, try making one of the recipes and share the yummy product with your friends or family. For an even greater challenge, try finding a recipe on the Internet or in a cookbook at your local library.

The Three Bears I

(Scatter Chart)

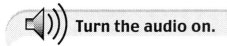 **Turn the audio on.**

Track 6

Tony: Well, I don't see how that really answers the clue. We still don't know where Juan Paco Pedro De la Mar eats his "chile."

Grandpa: Wait a minute. Say that again.

Tony: I said, we don't know where Juan Paco Pedro De la Mar—

Grandpa: That's it! I remember. When Don Diego used to sail into Cancun, he used to go to an old tavern called the "Chile De la Mar." That must be what the clue means.

Narrator: Your grandfather gets on the phone and makes some calls. He finds that the tavern is still standing although it has been renovated into a sidewalk cafe. Before you know it, you are in Grandpa's car, driving through the bustling city of Cancún. The car pulls up in front of a pleasant-looking little cafe.

Tony: This place doesn't look old enough for a pirate to have been here.

Grandpa: Yes, well, they must have changed it considerably. Let's hope there's enough of the original structure left to find what we're looking for.

Narrator: Your grandpa goes and speaks to the owner of the cafe, who shows him the one wall that is still standing from the original "Chile De la Mar." With a shrug, the three of you begin examining the wall.

Lisa: Grandpa! Tony! Look! Here, in this crack . . . it's the next clue!

Tony: Wow, that was close. Good thing they left that wall standing.

Grandpa: Yes. I'm surprised that we've been able to find all of the clues so far, after how long they've been hidden.

Narrator: Your grandpa orders you both some tortilla chips and guacamole, a tasty dip made from avocados. If you want to try to make guacamole, there is a recipe in the back of your workbook. You sit outside the cafe at a table and munch while you look over the next clue.

Lisa: It's another written clue. It says, "Encuentra los tres osos."

Grandpa: Oh, dear. I think I know which story that is referring to. It is a pretty difficult one.

Tony: Well, then, we'd better start learning it now.

Grandpa: You're right. Okay. Here are some new words you're going to need to know.

Look at the pictures on your workbook page and point to what you hear.

Track 7

los tres osos
the three bears

el dormitorio
the bedroom

rugió
roared

la cocina
the kitchen

el salón
the living room

el osito bebé
the baby bear

los platos hondos
the bowls

la cama
the bed

el oso mamá
the mother bear

la puerta
the door

el oso papá
the father bear

la silla
the chair

someone
alguien

la mesa
the table

la cuchara
the spoon

el mosh
the mush

 Turn the audio off.

Performance Challenge:

Choose five of the new words and pictures that you learned in the Scatter Chart. Show the pictures to a parent, friend, or one of your brothers and sisters and explain to them how you think the picture represents the words you have learned. For an even greater challenge, create your own story using the pictures. Bring out the artist in yourself by drawing your own versions of the pictographs and making a book with the story you create.

The Three Bears I

(Diglot Weave)

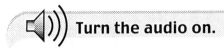 **Turn the audio on.**

Track 8

Narrator: You're still going over all of the new words that your grandpa has told you when you hear a voice from inside the cafe.

Malo: ¡No, no! ¡No me estás ayudando! Dije que necesito saber cuál parte del café. . .

Tony: Do you hear that?

Lisa: It sounds like Malo!

Narrator: You sneak over to the entrance of the cafe and look inside. You see a person speaking to the owner, but before you can get a good look at them, they see you and walk away quickly.

Tony: Do you really think it was Malo?

Lisa: I do. He's on the trail of the treasure!

Tony: Well, we'll just have to figure it out before he does.

Grandpa: That's right, Tony. We should go back to the hotel. While we're on the way, let me tell you a simple version of the story.

El cuento de los tres osos y Rizos de Oro

This is the famoso cuento about los tres osos y Rizos de Oro. As in other children's stories, este cuento begins with the words: había una vez . . . once upon a time. Now escucha el cuento.

Track 9

Había una vez tres osos. They lived en una 🏠 *en el* 🌳 *. If you know el*

📖 *, La ventana rota . . . The Broken Window, y el* 📖 *, Los tres cochinitos,*

you know what una 🏠 *is y what un* 🌳 *is. Un* 🌳 *es where los* 🐺 *y*

los 🐻 *and other* 🐕 *live, isn't it? Los tres* 🐻 *are el oso* 🐻 *, el oso*

🐻 *, y el osito* 🐻 *.*

One morning el 🐻 *, cooked up a nice pot of oatmeal* 🥣 *. Then she set la*

🪑 *with* 🥣 *y tres cucharas: un* 🥣 *grande, y una* 🥄 *grande para el* oso papá, un 🥣 mediano y una 🥄 mediana for herself, y un platito

y una cucharita para el 🐻 . She filled los 🥣🥣 with the hot mosh, y called

out, "¡Oso Papá, Osito Bebé, vengan a comer . . . come 'n eat!"

El 🐻 sat down at la 🪑, picked up his 🥄 grande y tasted el mosh en

su 🥣 grande. "¡Ay! Too hot, el mosh está too hot," él dijo. El 🐻 sat down

at la 🪑, picked up her 🥄 mediana y tasted the mosh en su 🥣 medi-

ano "¡Ay-ay! Sí, el 🥣 está too hot," ella dijo. El 🐻 sat down at la 🪑

picked up su 🥄 tasted el mosh. "Ay-ay! Sí, el 🥣 está too hot," él dijo.

Then el 🐻 dijo, "I say, let's go take a walk en el 🌳." El 🐻 dijo, "Oh,

yes, let's go take a walk en el 🌳." El 🐻 dijo: Oh, yes, let's go for a walk

en el 🌳." Then el 🐻, el oso mama y el osito 🐻 went out to take a

walk en el 🌳.

Pero they forgot to lock la 🚪 . Oh-oh!

Now, while los 🐻🐻🐻 were walking en el 🌳, una niñita came by. It was

Goldilocks. She saw la 🏠 de los 🐻 . Not knowing that it was la 🏠 de

los 🐻🐻🐻, she knocked on la 🚪 . No one came.

She opened la 🚪 y called out, "Yoo-hoo!" No one answered. So she entered en 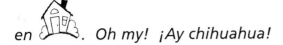. *Oh my!* ¡Ay chihuahua!

First she went into la [image] *. There she saw los* [image] *en la* [image] *. "I'm hungry,"*

ella dijo. *"Tengo hambre. I think no one will mind if I taste this* [image] *. Then*

Goldilocks sat down at la [image] *, took la* [image] *grande y tasted el* [image] *en el*

[image] *grande, el plato hondo del* [image] *. "¡Ay-ay! Este* [image] *está too hot," ella*

dijo. *Then she went over y took la* [image] *mediana tasted el* [image] *en el* [image]

mediano, el plato hondo del [image] *. "¡Ay-ay!" ella dijo, "este* [image] *está too*

hot." *Then she went over y took la* [image] *y tasted el* [image] *en el platito* [image]

del [image] *. "¡Ahhh!" ella dijo, este* [image] *está just right. And without thinking,*

Goldilocks ate it all up.

Then she went into the living room . . . el salón. There she vio tres [image] *una*

grande, la silla del [image] *; una* [image] *mediana, la silla del* [image] *; y una*

pequeñita, la silla del [image] *. First Goldilocks sat down on la* [image] *grande. "¡Ay!*

esta silla es too hard," ella dijo. Then she went over y sat down on la [image] *medi-*

ana. *"¡Ay! esta silla es too soft," ella dijo. Then she went over y sat down on la*

[image] *pequeñita, la silla del* [image] *. "¡Ah! esta* [image] *es just right," ella dijo. She*

leaned back y CRACK! la silla broke. What a pity! ¡Qué lástima!

She picked herself up and went upstairs to el dormitorio. There she vio tres

: una grande, la cama del ; una mediana, la cama del ; y una una pequeñita, la cama del . First Goldilocks lay down on la grande, la cama del . "¡Ay!" ella dijo, "esta es too hard."

Then she went over y sat down on la mediana, la cama del . "¡Ay! esta es too soft," ella dijo. Then she went over y lay down on la , la cama del . "¡Ah¡" ella dijo, "esta cama es just right, and I am very tired."

Then she laid her head on the pillow y soon fell asleep.

Just then los returned from their walk en el . First they went into la . There el vio su y dijo, "Oh-oh, somebody has tasted mi ." El vio su y dijo, "Oh-oh, has tasted el mío." El vio su y dijo, "Oh-oh, has tasted el mío, too, and has eaten it all up." Y el osito bebé began to cry (boo-hoo).

Then los tres went into el . El looked at su grande y , " has sat en mi ." El looked at su mediana y dijo, " has sat en la mía." El looked at su y dijo, has sat en la mía, too, and broke it. Look!" Y el osito bebé began to cry.

Then los went upstairs. El looked at su grande y ,

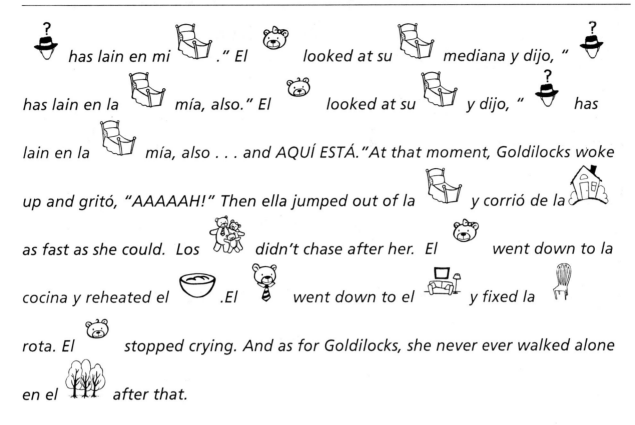 has lain en mi ⛺." El 🐻 looked at su 🛏 mediana y dijo, "

has lain en la 🛏 mía, also." El 🐻 looked at su 🛏 y dijo, " has

lain en la 🛏 mía, also . . . and AQUÍ ESTÁ." "At that moment, Goldilocks woke

up and gritó, "AAAAAH!" Then ella jumped out of la 🛏 y corrió de la 🏠

as fast as she could. Los 🐻🐻🐻 didn't chase after her. El 🐻 went down to la

cocina y reheated el 🥣 . El 🐻 went down to el 🛋 y fixed la 🪑

rota. El 🐻 stopped crying. And as for Goldilocks, she never ever walked alone

en el 🌳 after that.

 Turn the audio off.

Performance Challenge:

There are four parts to this Performance Challenge:

1. Read the story silently to yourself.
2. Read the story aloud to yourself.
3. Read the story aloud to a parent, friend or one of your brothers and sisters.
4. Retell the story in your own words, using as much Spanish as you can, to a parent, friend or one of your brothers and sisters.
Don't worry if you can't remember every word. Do the best you can, and review the audio if you need to.

For an even greater challenge, write the next chapter for each diglot weave. If the story hadn't ended, what would happen next?

The Three Bears I

(Review Questions)

  Turn the audio on.

Narrator: Your grandpa is tucking you in bed, but you are too nervous to sleep. Between having the hotel room broken into and seeing Malo at the cafe, you are not feeling very safe.

Lisa: Grandpa, will you stay with us until we fall asleep?

Grandpa: Yes, but you know you don't have to worry. Nothing will happen to you as long as I'm here.

Tony: I know, but still . . . I want to learn how to solve the clue as fast as I can.

Grandpa: Well, let's go over what we've learned so far. Do you remember all the story that I told you earlier?

Lisa: I think so.

Grandpa: Well, let's see if you can answer some questions. Then you must go to bed.

 True or False:

1. *El mosh de los tres osos está too hot to comer at first.*

2. *Goldilocks is una buena amiga de los tres osos.*

3. *It is un accidente when Goldilocks breaks la silla del osito bebé.*

4. *Los tres osos comen el bosque with milk for breakfast.*

5. *Los tres osos sleep en la cocina.*

6. *Goldilocks falls asleep en la cama del osito bebé.*

 Turn the audio off.

Answers: 1. T 2. F 3. T 4. F 5. F 6. T

The Three Bears II

(DiglotWeave)

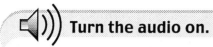 **Turn the audio on.**

Track 12

Narrator: You're feeling much better by morning, and Grandpa Glen begins to pack up your bags.

Lisa: Hey, Grandpa, are we leaving already?

Grandpa: We have no time to waste. If Malo knew enough to find the "Chile De la Mar," he's probably figured out where to go next.

Lisa: Do we even know where to go next?

Grandpa: Well, I've got a pretty good idea, but we'd better figure out as much of that puzzle as we can first. In case I'm wrong, we don't have time to backtrack. Do you think you are ready to learn the more advanced version of the story?

Tony: We'd better be. We don't have much time.

Grandpa: All right then.

El cuento de los tres osos and Rizos de Oro

Track 13

Here is the next level of el famoso cuento about los tres osos y la niñita named Goldilocks. In Spanish her nombre es Rizos de Oro. As in other children's stories, este cuento begins with the words: había una vez. Now escucha.

Había una vez tres osos. They lived en una casa en el bosque. If you remember el cuento La ventana rota. . .The Broken Window, y el cuento Los tres cochinitos, you know what una casa is y what el bosque is. Un bosque es where los lobos y los osos and other animals live, right? Los tres osos are el oso papá, el oso mamá, y el osito bebé.

One morning el oso mamá cooked up a pot of oatmeal mosh. Then she set la mesa with tres platos hondos y tres cucharas: un plato hondo grande y una cuchara grande para el oso papa, un plato hondo mediano y una cuchara mediana for herself, y un platito hondo y una cucharita para el osito bebé.

She filled los tres platos hondos with the hot mosh, y llamó: "¡Oso Papá, Osito Bebé, vengan a comer!"

El oso papá sat down at la mesa, picked up his cuchara grande y tasted el mosh en su plato hondo grande. "¡Ay! Too caliente, el mosh está too caliente," él dijo.

El oso mamá se sentó a la mesa, picked up her cuchara mediana y tasted el mosh en su plato hondo mediano. "¡Ay-ay! Sí, el mosh está demasiado caliente," ella dijo.

El osito bebé se sentó a la mesa, picked up su cucharita y probó el mosh. "Ay-ay! Demasiado caliente, el mosh está demasiado caliente," él dijo.

Then el oso papá dijo, "I say, let's take a walk en el bosque."

El oso mamá dijo, "O yes, let's take un paseo en el bosque."

El osito bebé dijo, "O sí, vamos a dar un paseo en el bosque."

Then el oso papa, el oso mama, y el osito bebé went out to dar un paseo en el bosque. Pero they forgot to lock la puerta.

Now, while los tres osos were taking un paseo en el bosque, una niñita came by. It was Rizos de Oro. She saw la casa de los tres osos. She didn't know that it was la casa de los tres osos. She knocked on la puerta. No one came a la puerta. She opened la puerta y llamó, "Yoo-hoo!" No one answered. So she entered en la casa.

First she went into la cocina. There she saw los tres platos hondos en la mesa. "I'm hungry," ella dijo. "Tengo hambre. I think no one will mind if I pruebo this mosh.

Then Rizos de Oro se sentó a la mesa, picked up la cuchara grande y probó el mosh en el plato hondo grande, el plato hondo del oso papá. "¡Ay-ay! Este mosh está demasiado caliente," ella dijo.

Then she went over and picked up la cuchara mediana y probó el mosh en el plato hondo mediano, el plato hondo del oso mamá. "¡Ay-ay!," ella dijo, "este mosh está demasiado caliente, too."

Then she went over & picked up la cucharita y probó el mosh en el platito hondo del osito bebé. "¡Aaaah!" ella dijo, "este mosh está just right." And without thinking, Rizos de Oro ate it all up . . . se lo comió todo.

Then she went into the living room . . . el salón. There she vio tres sillas: una silla grande, la silla del oso papá; una silla mediana, la silla del oso mamá; y una silla pequeñita, la silla del osito bebé.

First Rizos de Oro se sentó en la silla grande. "¡Ay! esta silla es demasiado dura," *ella dijo.*

Then she went over y se sentó en la silla mediana. "¡Ay! esta silla es demasiado suave," ella dijo.

Then she went over y se sentó en la silla pequeñita. "¡Aaaah! esta silla es just right," ella dijo. As she leaned back, la silla broke.

She picked herself up and went upstairs to the bedroom. There she vio tres camas: una cama grande, la cama del oso papá; una cama mediana, la cama del oso mamá; y una cama pequeñita, la cama del osito bebé.

First Rizos de Oro se acostó en la cama grande, la cama del oso papá. "¡Ay! esta cama es demasiado dura," ella dijo.

Then she went over y se acostó en la cama mediana. "¡Ay! esta cama es demasia-do suave," ella dijo.

Then she went over y se acostó en la cama pequeñita. "¡Aaaah!, esta cama es just right," ella dijo. Then she put her head on the pillow and soon se durmió.

Just then los osos returned from their paseo en el bosque. First they went into la cocina. There el oso papá vio su plato hondo y dijo, "Oh-oh, somebody has tasted mi mosh."

El oso mamá vio su plato hondo y dijo, "Oh-oh, alguien has tasted mi mosh, too."

El osito bebé vio su platito hondo y dijo, "Oh, alguien ha probado mi mosh, too, y se lo comió todo." Y el osito bebé began to llorar.

Then los tres osos went into el salón. El oso papá looked at su silla grande y rugió, "Someone has sat en mi silla."

El oso mamá vio su silla mediana y dijo, "Alguien has sat en la silla mía, too."

El osito bebé vio su silla pequeñita y dijo: "Alguien se ha sentado en la silla mía también, y la rompió." Y el osito bebé began to llorar (boo-hoo).

Then los tres osos went upstairs. El oso papá looked at su cama grande y rugió, Alguien has lain en mi cama."

El oso mamá looked at su cama mediana y dijo: "Alguien se ha acostado en la cama mía también."

El osito bebé looked at su cama pequeñita y dijo, "Alguien se ha acostado en la cama mía también, Y TODAVÍA ESTÁ AQUÍ."

Hearing this, Rizos de Oro se despertó. Seeing los osos, she gritó, "AAAAAH!"
She saltó de la cama y corrió de la casa.

And she never returned to la casa de los tres osos again.

 Turn the audio off.

Performance Challenge:

There are four parts to this Performance Challenge:
1. Read the story silently to yourself.
2. Read the story aloud to yourself.
3. Read the story aloud to a parent, friend or one of your brothers and sisters.
4. Retell the story in your own words, using as much Spanish as you can, to a parent, friend or one of your brothers and sisters.
Don't worry if you can't remember every word. Do the best you can, and review the audio if you need to.
For an even greater challenge, write the next chapter for each diglot weave. If the story hadn't ended, what would happen next?

The Three Bears II

(Story Telling)

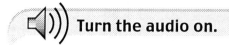 **Turn the audio on.**

Track 14

Narrator: Grandpa Glen is driving down the coast of the Caribbean. You can't contain your excitement any more.

Lisa: Please, please tell us where we're going, Grandpa Glen?

Grandpa Glen: Well, I remember from the memoirs of Don Diego that he spent some time outside of Tulum, on a hennequen farm. He called the farm "Los Tres Osos." Do you remember what that means?

Tony: Of course. That means, "The Three Bears." Like in the story.

Grandpa Glen: Right. Well, the farm he lived in is still there. In fact, it was from the owner of the farm that I first bought Don Diego's memoirs.

Lisa: What sort of farm did you say it was?

Grandpa: Hennequen. It's a plant that they grow here on the Yucatán peninsula to make rope and twine. It looks a little bit like an aloe plant, but much bigger.

Tony: Cool. It's a good thing you know the owner of the farm; that will give us an advantage over Malo.

Grandpa: That's right, but we'll need more of an advantage than that. Do you remember the story from this morning?

Lisa: Of course we do!

Grandpa: Good. Repeat it back to me in Spanish, to make sure that you have it all.

Now retell the story, using as much Spanish as you can.

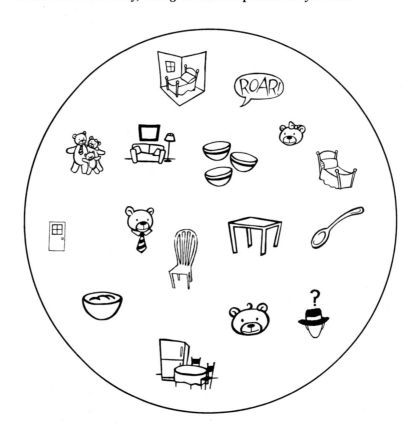

Turn the audio off.

Word Puzzle 1

(*The Three Bears*)

Turn the audio on.

Narrator: Grandpa Glen turns his car into a long driveway that winds through a large hennequen farm.

Lisa: Is that hennequen?

Grandpa: Yes, it is. It is a very important export here.

Tony: Wow. It's kind of funny looking, like a big green octopus.

Narrator: Finally, you come within sight of the house. A tall, thin man is standing out front.

Grandpa: ¡Hola! ¡Hola, Pedro! ¿Te acuerdas de mí? Soy Glen.

Pedro: ¡Oh, Glen! ¡Qué sorpresa!

Narrator: Your grandfather introduces you to Pedro, the owner of the farm.

Pedro: Mucho gusto. Adelante.

Narrator: Your grandpa tells Pedro all about the treasure hunt that the memoirs have led him on, and Pedro agrees to help you search the farm. You all go outside together and begin to walk around the mansion.

Tony: We'll never find it. The farm is too big.

Narrator: Just then, you see a tiled mural on one of the outside walls of the house.

Tony: Hey, do you guys see that?

Lisa: Yeah, what is it?

Pedro: ¡Oh, claro! Me había olvidado de este mural viejo.

Grandpa: It looks like three bears, all lined up just like in the story. Good work, children!

Narrator: You all begin to search the mural for a clue.

Lisa: Look! There're two pieces of parchment slid in this crack.

Pedro: Bien hecho. Glen, ahora veo por qué necesitas a los niños.

Grandpa: Yes, they're both a big help. Let me see the parchment. Interesting. This first one looks like another word puzzle. Let's see if we can solve it.

Turn the audio off.

Fill in the blanks in the puzzle below by following the numbered clues. The letters that fall in the circled blanks will make an additional word that will help you on your adventure.

1. I taste

2.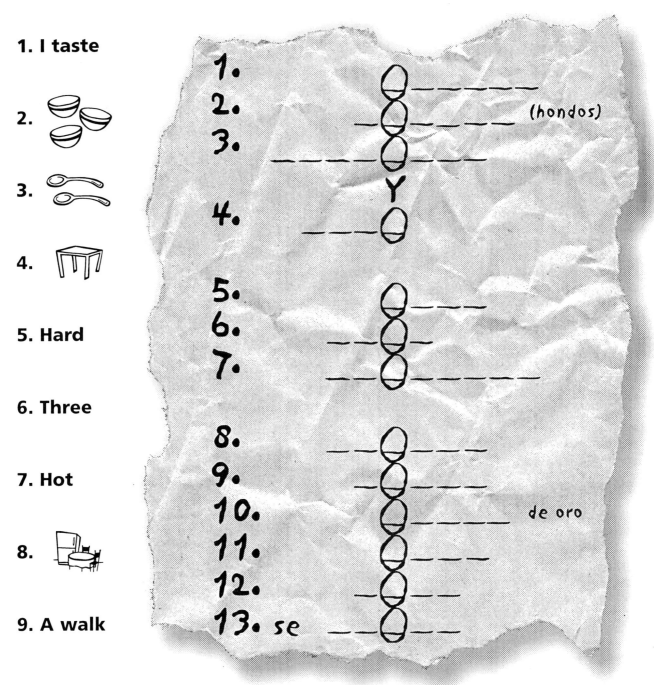

3.

4.

5. Hard

6. Three

7. Hot

8.

9. A walk

10. Goldilocks

11.   **12.**   **13. She sat down**

The Dog, the Cat, and the Mouse I
(Scatter Chart)

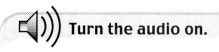 **Turn the audio on.**

Tony: Okay, so the puzzle says, "Playa del Carmen." What does that mean?

Grandpa: Well, Playa del Carmen is a very famous beach not very far from here.

Lisa: What is on the second piece of parchment?

Grandpa: It looks like some sort of drawing ripped in half.

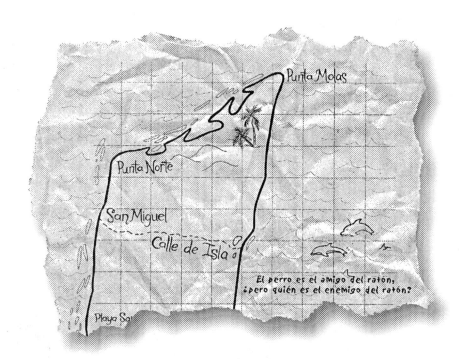

Grandpa: And look, here on the bottom is what looks like a riddle. Let's see. "El perro es el amigo del ratón, ¿pero quién es el enemigo del ratón?"

Tony: What does it mean, Grandpa?

Grandpa: I believe it refers to a story that I remember from my folklore research. It's a little bit difficult, however. You'll need to learn some new vocabulary. Okay?

Look at the pictures on your workbook page and point to what you hear.

Track 17

el piso
the floor

buenos amigos
good friends

la estufa
the stove

el hueco
the hole

atrapar
to trap

oler
to smell

la pared
the wall

el techo
the roof

busca
searches

medianoche
midnight

Turn the audio off.

Performance Challenge:

Choose five of the new words and pictures that you learned in the Scatter Chart. Show the pictures to a parent, friend, or one of your brothers and sisters and explain to them how you think the picture represents the words you have learned. For an even greater challenge, create your own story using the pictures. Bring out the artist in yourself by drawing your own versions of the pictographs and making a book with the story you create.

The Dog, the Cat, and the Mouse I

(Diglot Weave)

Turn the audio on.

Track 18

Grandpa: Okay, we should go then, to make sure that we get to the Playa del Carmen before Malo does. Gracias, Pedro.

Tony & Lisa: Si, Gracias.

Pedro: De nada. ¡Buena suerte!

Narrator: You both sit in the car with your grandpa, thinking about everything that has happened.

Tony: Grandpa? Do you think that we're ready to hear the new story now?

Grandpa: Yes, now would be a good time to tell it, before we arrive at La Playa del Carmen. Listen.

El perro, el gato, y el ratón

Track 19

Un ratón, un gato, y un perro viven together under the same techo en España. They live in una casa like la casa donde vives tú. Even though los animales hablan diferentes languages, el gato y el perro son buenos amigos.

Pero el gato no es amigo del ratón. El gato es Enemigo Número Uno. Cuando el gato ve al ratón, él tries to atraparlo. El wants to comerlo, pero el ratón always escapa. El ratón corre a su hole en la wall debajo de la stove.

There inside de la hole en la pared debajo de la estufa es donde vive el ratón. Es cómodo y safe there. El gato can squeeze debajo de la estufa, pero él is demasiado grande para entrar en el hueco donde always escapa el ratón cuando el gato tries to atraparlo.

El ratón duerme durante el día, pero a medianoche, cuando es dark, y todos están dormidos, y él can escuchar que todo está quieto, el ratón leaves su hueco y busca comida en la cocina. El looks en todas direcciones sniffing por algo para comer, some pedazo de comida que alguien has left out o dropped en el piso. Best of all es cuando he can oler queso, especialmente queso suizo, pero él come any tipo de queso. En la noche, as much as he likes to buscar comida en la cocina, él always has to watch out for el gato.

El doesn't have to watch out del perro, porque el perro es su buen amigo. Even though they hablan diferentes idiomas, son buenos amigos. Son such buenos amigos que sometimes, cuando el perro wakes up a medianoche y wants to play, él goes a la cocina, sticks su nariz debajo de la estufa y ladra softly, "arf,arf," invitando a su pequeño amigo a salir y play. Y el ratón, knowing que he is safe con el perro, sale de su hueco y corre por toda la casa con el perro while everyone else duermen.

Una noche el ratón estaba escuchando to make sure que no one was awake, y que él could salir de su hueco y buscar something para comer. Suddenly escuchó a faint sound outside de su hueco: "arf,arf." "Oh," él pensó, "es mi amigo el perro. Voy a salir para play con él." Excited, salió corriendo de su hueco y el gato lo atrapó con los sharp claws. El gato, con el ratón atrapado by la cola, saw him y dijo, "arf,arf."

Now you see how useful it is to saber another idioma.

El pobre ratón thought, "If only I knew como hablar like un león o un perro, el gato would be scared y yo could escapar." But el ratón didn't know el idioma de los leones, nor el idioma de los perros. Solo sabía el idioma de los ratones.

La only thing that él could dijo before the end came was, "Eek,eek"

 Turn the audio off.

Performance Challenge:

There are four parts to this Performance Challenge:
1. Read the story silently to yourself.
2. Read the story aloud to yourself.
3. Read the story aloud to a parent, friend or one of your brothers and sisters.
4. Retell the story in your own words, using as much Spanish as you can, to a parent, friend or one of your brothers and sisters. Don't worry if you can't remember every word. Do the best you can, and review the audio if you need to.
For an even greater challenge, write the next chapter for each diglot weave. If the story hadn't ended, what would happen next?

The Dog, the Cat, and the Mouse I

(Review Questions)

  Turn the audio on.

Narrator: When you arrive at the Playa del Carmen, you are amazed at how crowded the beach is.

Lisa: Grandpa, look! There must be a thousand people here. How will we ever find anything?

Grandpa: Well, that's a good question. We need to find something that has to do with the clue. Do you remember the clue? It's, "El perro es el amigo del ratón, pero quién es el enemigo del ratón?"

Tony: Well, we should figure out what the answer to the clue is then.

Grandpa: How much of the story do you remember? Do you think that you could answer some review questions?

Lisa: Sure.

Tony: I think so.

Grandpa: Okay. Listen.

True or False

1. El perro es buen amigo del ratón.

2. El gato lives en un hueco en la pared debajo de la estufa.

3. El ratón sleeps during la noche.

4. El ratón likes to comer queso.

5. El gato tricks el ratón.

 Turn the audio off.

Answers: 1.T 2.F 3.F 4.T 5.T

The Dog, the Cat, and the Mouse II

(Diglot Weave)

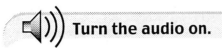 **Turn the audio on.**

Narrator: The sun is blazing hot, and you are all very thirsty. Your grandpa leaves you in the shade of a beach umbrella while he goes to buy some lemonade.

Tony: Well, we did pretty well on those review questions. All we need to do now is learn the whole story so we can solve the riddle.

Lisa: Yeah. I hope it won't be too hard.

Tony: I don't think that-- Lisa, duck!

Narrator: You both quickly duck behind the umbrella.

Lisa: What is it, Tony?

Tony: I think I saw Malo out there!

Lisa: Are you sure?

Narrator: You both cautiously peek out behind the rim of the umbrella, and you see Malo standing not ten feet away from you! He looks hot and uncomfortable, and he is speaking to a person on the beach.

Malo: ¿Está seguro? Estoy buscando algún tipo de perro, o ratón, o gato. ¿Sabe ustéd dónde se encuentra uno de éstos?

Narrator: You both hide behind the umbrella again.

Tony: Hey! I recognized some of those words. "Perro" and "ratón" and "gato."

Lisa: He must be looking for the clue. We have to beat him to it!

Grandpa: What are you hiding from, children?

Tony: Quick, Grandpa, duck! Malo's out there and he might see you.

Grandpa: Well, if he was here he's gone now.

Lisa: Do you think he saw you?

Grandpa: I don't know. Well, if he's here then he hasn't found the clue yet, and we still have a chance to get it.

Tony: Hurry, Grandpa, and tell us the story now. Please?

Grandpa: Okay. Listen.

El perro, el gato, y el ratón

Track 23

Un ratón, un gato, y un perro viven juntos bajo el mismo techo en España. Es una casa como la casa donde vives tú. Aunque los animales hablan diferentes idiomas, el gato y el perro son buenos amigos.

Pero el gato no es amigo del ratón. El gato es Enemigo Número Uno. Cuando el gato ve al ratón, él intenta atraparlo. El quiere comerlo, pero el ratón siempre escapa; el ratón corre a su hueco en la pared debajo de la estufa.

Allí, adentro del hueco debajo de la estufa, es donde vive el ratón. Es cómodo y seguro allí. El gato puede meterse debajo de la estufa, pero es demasiado grande para entrar en el hueco donde siempre escapa el ratón cuando el gato intenta atraparlo.

El ratón duerme durante el día, pero a medianoche, cuando es oscuro y todos están dormidos, y él puede escuchar que todo está quieto, el ratón sale de su hueco y busca comida en la cocina. El mira en todas direcciones husmeando por algo para comer, algún pedazo de comida que alguien haya tirado o dejado en el piso. Lo mejor es cuando puede oler queso, especialmente queso suizo, pero él come cualquier tipo de queso. En la noche, por más que le gustaba buscar comida en la cocina, siempre tiene que tener cuidado del gato.

El no tiene que cuidarse del perro, porque el perro es su buen amigo. Aunque hablan diferentes idiomas, son buenos amigos. Son tan buenos amigos que a veces cuando el perro despierta a medianoche y quiere jugar, él va a la cocina, apunta su nariz debajo de la estufa y ladra suavemente, "arf, arf" invitando a su pequeño amigo a salir y jugar. Y el ratón, sabiendo que es seguro con el perro, sale de su hueco y corre por toda la casa con el perro mientras duermen los demás.

Una noche, el ratón estaba escuchando por estar seguro de que no había nadie despierto para que el pudiera salir de su hueco y buscar algo para comer. De repente escuchó un ruido suave por fuera de su hueco, "arf, arf." "O," él pensó, "es mi amigo, el perro. Voy a salir a jugar con él." Animado, salió corriendo de su hueco y el gato lo atrapó con las garras. El gato, con el ratón atrapado por la cola, lo miró y dijo, "arf, arf."

Ahora ves lo útil que es saber otro idioma.

El pobre ratón pensó, "Sí solo supiera cómo hablar como un león o un perro, el gato tendría miedo y yo podría escapar." Pero el ratón no había aprendido el idioma de los leones, ni el idioma de los perros. Solo sabía el idioma de los ratones.

La única cosa que pudo decir antes del fin era, "Eek, eek!"

 Turn the audio off.

The Dog, the Cat, and the Mouse I

(Story Telling)

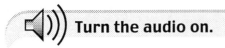 **Turn the audio on.**

Narrator: After looking around carefully to make sure that Malo is really gone, you all three begin to search the beach again, looking for the clue.

Grandpa: Okay. Let's listen to the clue again. "El perro es el amigo del ratón ¿pero quién es el enemigo del ratón?"

Lisa: So. "El perro es el amigo del ratón." That's from the story, and it means that the dog is friends with the mouse. Right?

Tony: Right. The second part is a question, "¿pero quién es el enemigo del ratón?" "Enemigo" means enemy, so . . .

Lisa: So, if they want to know the "enemigo del ratón," it would be . . .

Tony: The cat! "El gato."

Grandpa: Good work, children. We need to look for a gato.

Narrator: You continue to search the beach. After a while you are hot and thirsty and beginning to wonder if you will ever find it.

Lisa: Let's go up to that old building and rest.

Tony: Yeah. I'm exhausted.

Narrator: Just as you begin to sit down on the porch of the building, under the shade of the doorway, you notice something odd.

Tony: Hey, Lisa, do you see that?

Lisa: Yeah! The tiles on the porch look like they make a picture.

Tony: It's the "gato!"

Grandpa: You're right. Now let's see if we can find the clue.

Narrator: You find a loose tile, and when you remove it, you find a piece of parchment with a puzzle on it and another piece of parchment, ripped.

Tony: What's this?

Grandpa: Hmmm. It looks like a drawing of some sort, but we only have half of it. What about the puzzle?

Lisa: Uh-oh. It looks pretty hard.

Grandpa: Yes, it does. We might need to review the story. Why don't you children tell the story back to me, to make sure you remember it all.

Now retell the story in your own words, using as much Spanixh as possible.

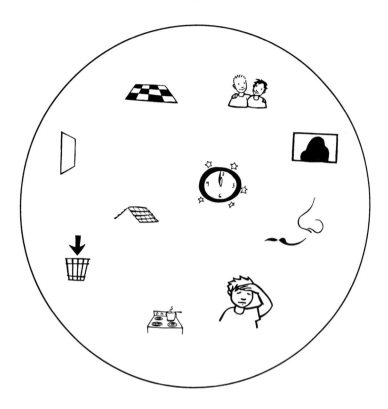

 Turn the audio off.

Word Puzzle 2

(The Dog, the Cat, and the Mouse)

Track 25

 Turn the audio on.

Grandpa: Good job, children. Now, let's see if we can do that puzzle.

Lisa: I'm so excited. If we found the puzzle that means that we're going to beat Malo to the treasure.

Grandpa: Well, not necessarily. Malo has the pirate's memoirs, and he might be able to figure out where to go next without the puzzle. It took us a long time to find it. He might already be on his way to the next location.

Tony: You're right, Grandpa. We don't even know where to go.

Grandpa: Well, let's solve the puzzle and see where it takes us.

Turn the audio off.

1.
2. **trap it**
3.
4. **medium**
5.
6.
7. **good**
8.
9.

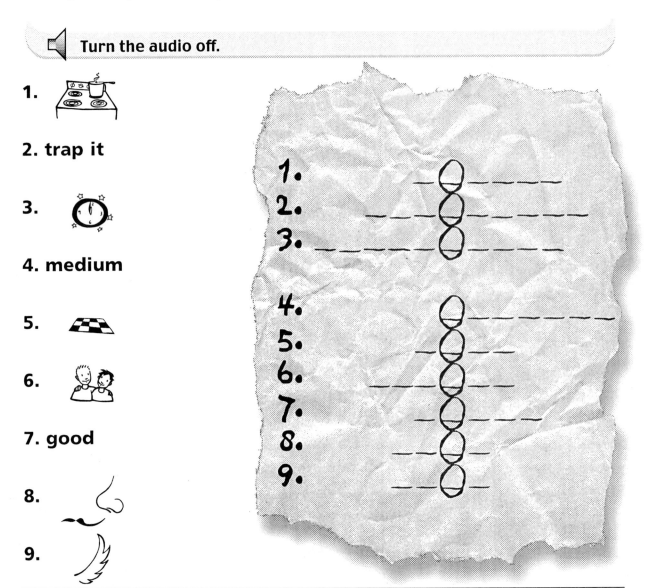

Hard Days

(Horseshoe Story)

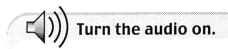 **Turn the audio on.**

Track 26

Lisa: Okay, the puzzle says "San Miguel." Where's that?

Grandpa: San Miguel is a town on the island of Cozumel, which is just off of the coast here. De Consuelo sometimes lived there during the stormy seasons. If I remember correctly, we should be able to catch a ferry there right from this beach.

Narrator: An hour later you are seated on the ferry in Grandpa's car. The island of Cozumel is approaching quickly, and you are amazed at how beautiful and green it is, floating on the blue ocean.

Tony: Where do you think we need to go in San Miguel, Grandpa?

Grandpa: Well, the place that Don Diego used to stay was outside of town. Let me look at the map of Cozumel . . . yes. It looks like it would have been right around here, which is now a marine park. It's called Chankanaab.

Lisa: Good! I can't wait!

Grandpa: De Consuelo's house was called "Días Duros," named after one of his favorite stories. I would guess, that if he is leading us there, he'll use that story in his next clue. Would you like to hear it?

Tony: Yeah! We'll beat Malo yet.

Grandpa Glen: Días duros para mi hermano menor:

"Días Duros"

1. *Hace tres días . . . mi hermano se cayó y se rompió el brazo.*
2. *Anteayer . . . por accidente se cortó con un cuchillo.*
3. *Ayer . . . se quemó la mano.*
4. *Hoy . . . se enfermó y se desmayó.*
5. *Mañana . . . yo espero que él verá al doctor.*
6. *Pasado mañana . . . pienso que irá al hospital.*
7. *En dos o tres días más . . . espero que él estará bien.*

 Turn the audio off.

Performance Challenge:

Create hand actions to represent the actions in the horseshoe story. (For example: Make up different actions to represent the animals you heard about in the story.) After you have created the actions, perform your mini-play for a parent, friend, or one of your bothers and sisters. Remember to narrate your actions in Spanish and then translate your words if your audience does not understand Spanish. For an even greater challenge, try writing your own horseshoe story. Choose several things or people that are related to each other in some way. Think of a chain of events that connects the characters in the story. To finish the story, figure out how the events could be reversed in order to back through the pictures and the plot.

Hard Days

(Scatter Chart)

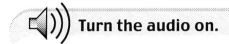 **Turn the audio on.**

Track 28

Narrator: You arrive on the island of Cozumel and immediately begin driving to Chankanaab. It is getting later in the afternoon, and you want to find the next clue before night.

Grandpa: Okay. I picked up a brochure on this place, Chankanaab. and It looks pretty exciting. It's a marine park with dolphins and a lagoon. There is also a replica of an ancient Mayan village, and I think that's where we'll find "Días Duros."

Lisa: Great! I still don't know some of the words for "Días Duros," though.

Grandpa: Okay, Lisa. Let's go over the new words before we get there.

Look at the pictures on your workbook page and point to what you hear..

Turn the audio off.

Performance Challenge:

Choose five of the new words and pictures that you learned in the Scatter Chart. Show the pictures to a parent, friend, or one of your brothers and sisters and explain to them how you think the picture represents the words you have learned. For an even greater challenge, create your own story using the pictures. Bring out the artist in yourself by drawing your own versions of the pictographs and making a book with the story you create.

Hard Days

(Story Telling)

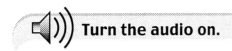 **Turn the audio on.**

Track 30

Narrator: You arrive at the park of Chankanaab. It is a fascinating place, and you wish that you could spend more time there. You walk past the dolphins and are amazed to see that they let people right inside with them so they can play and swim.

Tony: Wow. Will you look at all of those people?

Lisa: Yeah. Hey! Tony, Grandpa! Isn't that Malo, over there?

Malo: Estoy buscando una casa que se llama "Días Duros".

Grandpa: You're right! Quick children, let's run for the village as fast as we can!

Narrator: While Malo asks around for directions, you both run after your grandfather, and you hope his map helps you find the hut. After looking at the huts, Grandpa points one out.

Grandpa: I think this must be "Días Duros."

Narrator: You duck inside the hut and look around. There is almost nothing there except a hammock and a fire pit.

Tony: Now what? Malo could be here any moment.

Grandpa: Well, let's think. What does it say in the story? Do you remember? Let's go over the story again. Tell it to me, so I can see how much you know.

Now retell the story, using as much Spanish as you can.

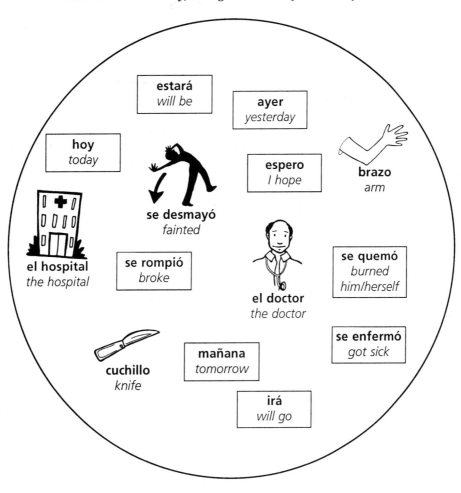

Turn the audio off.

The Mystery Map

(Cozumel)

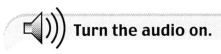 **Turn the audio on.**

Tony: Wait a minute, Grandpa. One of the things that happened in the story is that the brother "se quemó la mano," right?

Lisa: The fire pit! It must be in the fire pit!

Narrator: Quickly, you begin searching the old pit. The pit is surrounded by heavy stones, and as you look underneath one, you find a piece of parchment.

Grandpa: This must be it. What is it?

Tony: It looks like another drawing, ripped up.

Grandpa: Wait! Let's put the two together. See? They make a map! It looks like the island of Cozumel.

Lisa: It must be showing where the treasure is hidden. How will we know where to look?

Grandpa: Well, there're directions printed here. Let's see if we can figure it out.

 Turn the audio off.

1.) Rizos de Oro breaks a chair.
True: move down one space
False: move right two spaces

2.) El gato and el ratón are friends.
True: move down three spaces
False: move right one space

3.) Miércoles is the Spanish word for Monday.
True: move left one space
False: move right one space

4.) Little brother falls from a tree and breaks his brazo.
True: move up one space
False: move down two spaces

5.) El ratón lives under la estufa.
True: move right one space
False: move up one space

6.) Little brother burns his foot.
True: move down two spaces
False: move down three spaces

7.) Osito Bebé cries a lot.
True: move left one spaces
False: move right three spaces

8.) Mártes is the Spanish word for Tuesday.
True: move down one space
False: move up one space

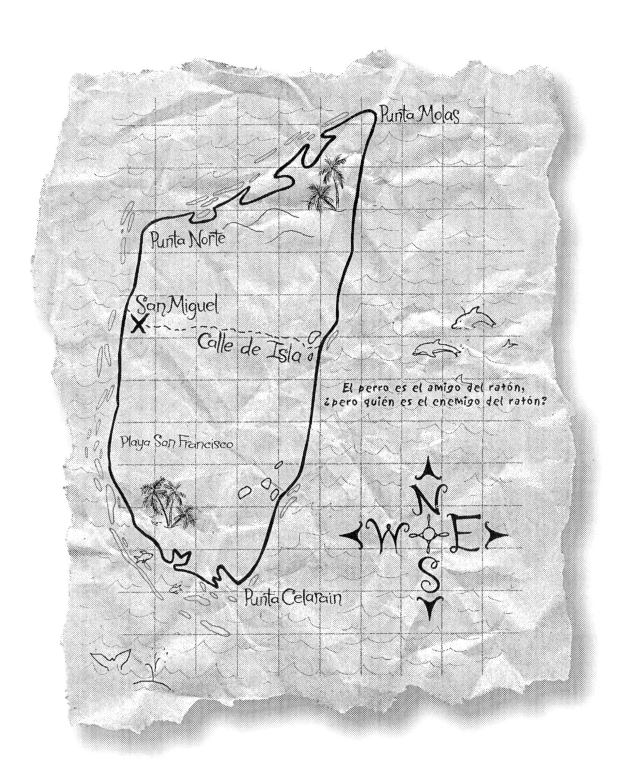

Treasure!

(Success)

  Turn the audio on.

Track 2

Narrator: Armed with the map, you leave the hut and begin walking back to the park entrance. You are nearly there when you hear a familiar voice behind you.

Malo: ¡Esperen! ¡Esperen! ¡Paren esos niños!

Lisa: It's Malo!

Tony: He's seen us!

Grandpa: Quick, children, run to the car as fast as you can! We have to find that treasure, now!

Narrator: You all pile into the car and your grandpa begins driving away, leaving an angry Malo behind you. You are so excited you can barely sit still as your grandpa tries to drive the car as close to the place marked on the map as possible.

Grandpa: Okay, this is probably as good as we can do. Let's get out and look.

Narrator: You all begin to wander through the dense jungle, looking for anything out of the ordinary. You get deeper and deeper, and farther from the safety of the road. You approach a small river, which twists through the brush.

Tony: Wait! Wait! Lisa, Grandpa! Do you see that? Over there, in the river. It looks like a small island. Do you think that might be where he hid the treasure?

Narrator: The island is very small, only a cluster of rocks in the stream. Holding onto your grandpa's hand, you wade into the churning water. The flow of the river tugs at your legs, and you have to be very careful to keep your balance. The water is nearly as deep as your chin by the time you reach the rocks, and your grandpa has to pull you up, wet and shivering.

Grandpa: Well, I'm not sure if there's anything here.

Lisa: Look, Grandpa! Between the two rocks, there's a little hollow. Let's check inside.

Narrator: You all clamber between the rocks and peer in. There, lying in piles, is the treasure. There are clay pots with beautiful designs visible on them beneath the layers of dust. Old, cracked leather pouches spill ancient gold and silver coins onto the ground, and a half-rotted Spanish tapestry is still draped over a rock. Perhaps the most brilliant piece, however, is the one least affected by the years. It is a gorgeous jade statue. The deep green stone has been carved into a snarling jaguar, ready to pounce.

Lisa: I can't believe it! We did it!

Tony: We found the treasure!

 Turn the audio off.

Test 1

(Review)

Track 3

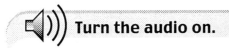 **Turn the audio on.**

Narrator: It is now a week later. You are sitting in Grandpa's living room in Progreso, right where your adventure began. The newspapers and the news on TV have all carried the story of the heroes who found all of the lost Mayan treasure and returned it to the state of Yucatán. Your parents are very proud.

Tony: And do you know what the best thing is? I haven't seen Malo once since this whole thing ended.

Lisa: Yeah, I guess.

Tony: What's wrong?

Lisa: I don't know. I guess I don't trust Malo. Where has he gone? He really wanted that treasure, Tony. I don't think he's going to give up.

Tony: Oh, come on. What could he possibly do now?

Narrator: Just then, your grandpa comes into the room. You take one look at his face, and you know something is very, very wrong.

Lisa: What happened?

Grandpa: Listen, children. This is very serious. Last night, Malo broke into the museum where the treasure was being kept and he stole that beautiful statue of the green jaguar. That piece was more valuable than all the rest of the treasure put together.

Tony: No! Not after all our hard work!

Grandpa: I'm afraid it's true.

Lisa: What are we going to do?

Grandpa: Well, I'm gonna to follow him, and try to get it back. I know a man, Malo's cousin, named Bruno. Malo has asked Bruno to help him sneak the treasure out of the country, but Bruno is a good man and called to tell me. Malo thinks that Bruno is still helping him, but he's really waiting for a chance to help us get the treasure back. Malo told Bruno that he was going to take the treasure to Costa Rica.

Tony: Costa Rica? When are we going?

Grandpa: No, no. It's getting far too dangerous for you to come with me. As much as I love your help, I think I should go alone.

Lisa: Grandpa, please let us come with you! Aren't we helping enough?

Grandpa: You have been a tremendous help.

Tony: Then let us come! Besides, think how much new Spanish we could learn if we went to another country.

Grandpa: Well . . .

Lisa: Please? Think of how much we have already learned.

Grandpa: Okay. If you can show your parents and me how much Spanish you've learned, I'll let you come to Costa Rica with me. But I'd better be impressed!

A. Frame Identifications

For each question, you will see a box with pictures. You will hear a statement about one of the pictures. There will be a pause of 10 seconds to identify the picture, and then the statement will be repeated.

1.

2.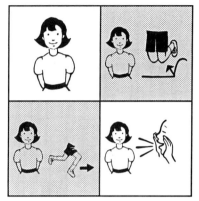

3.

4.

5.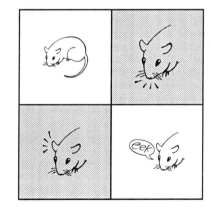

Comprehension Multiple-Choice

Answer the following questions by choosing the best answer or response.

1. "Todos tienen hambre."

    A. Vamos a dar un paseo en la selva.

    B. Muy bien, gracias.

    C. Vamos a comer.

    D. Si, es muy sabio.

2. Who owned la silla mediana?

    A. oso mamá

    B. oso papá

    C. osito bebé

    D. Rizos de Oro

3. What was wrong with Oso papa's mosh?

    A. demasiado suave

    B. demasiado pequeñita

    C. demasiado dura

    D. demasiado caliente

4. Why did el ratón come out a medianoche?

    A. para jugar con el gato

    B. para buscar algo para comer

    C. para dormir en la cocina

    D. para entrar en el hueco

5. ¿Cuándo verá tú hermano al doctor?

    A. Hace tres días

    B. Anteayer

    C. Ayer

    D. En dos o tres días más

 Turn the audio off.

Matching

Choose the statements that match and draw a line to connect the two.

1. bed	A. cuchara
2. stove	B. silla
3. chair	C. cama
4. bowl	D. estufa
5. spoon	E. plato hondo

True or False

Write T or F for each statement.

_____ 1. Los tres osos comieron a Goldilocks con leche por el desayuno.

_____ 2. Fue un accidente cuando Goldilocks rompió una silla.

_____ 3. El gato hizo una broma con el ratón.

_____ 4. El perro fue buen amigo del ratón.

_____ 5. Al ratón le gustaba comer queso.

Answer Key

1.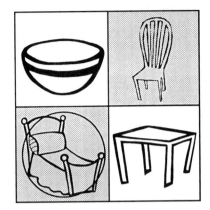

2.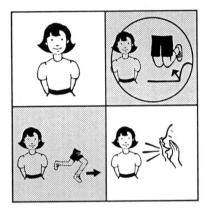

3.

4.

5.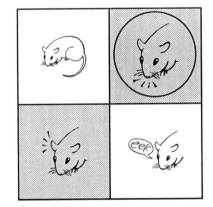

Comprehension Multiple-Choice

1. C. Vamos a comer.

2. A. oso mamá

3. D. demasiado caliente

4. B . buscar algo para comer

5. D. En dos o tres días más

Matching

1. C

2. D

3. B

4. E

5. A

True or False

1. F

2. T

3. T

4. T

5. T

The Adventure Continues

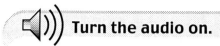 **Turn the audio on.**

Track 6

Narrator: Grandpa Glen has taken you down to Costa Rica, away from Yucatán, to try and track down Malo, who has disappeared with an extremely valuable statue from Don Diego's stash, which you helped find. Your plane lands in San José on a rainy, warm morning.

Tony: Where are we going again, Grandpa?

Grandpa: Ah, well, Bruno, Malo's cousin, said that he would call me at our hotel tonight and give me a place to meet him. He wants to do the right thing, I think, and return the statue, but he doesn't want Malo to get in trouble. I suspect he'll try to sneak the statue to me without Malo finding out. So, let's go and check into the hotel.

Narrator: You all climb into a cab and begin driving through San José. It is a lovely, friendly city, with everyone smiling and waving.

Tony: Wow! People seem really friendly here.

Grandpa: Yes, Tony, people from Costa Rica, "Ticos", they're called, are generally very friendly to strangers. I think you'll like this country.

Narrator: You arrive at a gorgeous hotel in the colonial Spanish style and check into your rooms.

Lisa: Look at this view! You can see the whole city from up here.

Tony: Do you really think that we'll be able to find the statue out there, Grandpa?

Grandpa: Well, it won't be easy.

Lisa: Don't worry, we'll be here to help you.

Grandpa: Yes, but only if you can use all of the Spanish you've learned. Not only that, but you need to learn much more as well. It will be a real challenge.

Tony: Come on! We can do it.

Grandpa: Can you? Are you willing to prove it?

Lisa: Sure. How?

Grandpa: Well, we have awhile to wait until Bruno gets a message to us. I have a puzzle that I made up to challenge my students. Do you think you could do it?

Tony: We can try!

Lisa: Yeah, let us see it!

 Turn the audio off.

Performance Challenge:

Well you're on your way to Costa Rica! Find an atlas, encyclopedia, or search on the Internet to find a detailed map of Costa Rica. Locate the capital city and find out as much as you can about local customs, dress, and pastimes.

Puzzle 1 - Rompecabezas 1

Start (time) _____

(Task 1): In this puzzle, the Spanish sentences are written without word space. Your task is to discover the Spanish words that match the English. Carefully compare the English sentences with the Spanish and mark the word division.

1. A dog sees a cat.

2. The cat sees the dog.

3. The dog says, "CAT."

4. The cat jumps.

5. The dog laughs.

1. Unperroveungato.

2. Elgatoveelperro.

3. Elperrodice"¡GATO!"

4. Elgatosalta.

5. Elperroserie.

(Task 2). Write the Spanish words that match the English (2) Vocabulary

cat __ __ __ __

dog __ __ __ __ __

a __ __

the __ __

sees __ __

says __ __ __ __

jumps __ __ __ __ __

laughs __ __ __ __ __

(Task 3). Write the words of the same five sentences

1 Un _____ _____ _____ _____

2 El _____ _____ _____ _____

3 El _____ _____ "_____!"

4 _____ _____ _____

5 _____ _____ _____

Answer Key:

(1) Word divisions marked
1 Un/perro/ve/un/gato.
2 El/gato/ve/el/perro.
3 El/perro/dice/"GATO!"
4 El/gato/salta.
5 El/perro/serie.

(2) Vocabulary
cat—gato
dog—perro
a—un
the—el
sees—ve
says—dice
jumps—salta
laughs—se rie

(3) Written sentence with word space
1 Un perro ve un gato.
2 El gato ve el perro.
3 El perro dice "GATO!"
4 El gato salta.
5 El perro serie.

Elapsed Time _____ minutos

Happy Birthday

(Ditties)

  Turn the audio on.

Track 7 **Narrator:** Just then, the phone rings.

Grandpa: Hola? . . . Sí, él habla . . . Claro. Estaré allí en seguida.

Lisa: Was that Bruno, Grandpa?

Grandpa: Yes it was. He said he will meet me in the national archives.

Tony: What's an archive?

Grandpa: It's a building where they store historical documents and public records. I used to do some of my folklore research there.

Lisa: Great! Let's go!

Narrator: You take a cab through the city until you reach the University of Costa Rica. Once there, your grandpa shows you around the archive.

Grandpa: Here's the folklore section, where I do research. I guess Bruno's not here yet.

Tony: That's okay. It gives us some time to look around.

Narrator: You begin to quietly explore the archives. It is like a large library, and all the books are very old. While your grandpa examines some old maps, you both look at some books on the shelf.

Tony: Wait! Lisa . . . do you hear that?

Malo: [faintly]Vamos. No quiero quedarme aquí más.

Lisa: It's Malo! Quick! Grandpa! Grandpa!

Narrator: You grab your grandfather and hurry over to where you heard the voice, but the aisle is empty. A large book lies open on the table. You all begin to look at it.

Grandpa: I wonder if Bruno left this.

Tony: Maybe it's some sort of clue.

Grandpa: Maybe.

Lisa: Will you teach it to us?

Grandpa: Of course. This is a birthday song. I first learned it a year ago on my birthday when Marcela and her parents threw a party for me. In the morning, they sent a mariachi, which is a group of musicians, over to my house to sing it to me. That night we hung a piñata filled with candy. We all took turns being blindfolded and hitting the piñata with a stick until it broke. Then we ate the candy. It's a wonderful song. Here's the first part:

    Feliz, feliz en tu día,   *(Happiness on your day,)*

Amiguito, que Dios te bendiga!	*(Friend, may God bless you!)*
Que reine la paz en tu día,	*(May peace reign on your day,)*
Y que cumplas muchos más!	*(And have many more)*

The second part has words that are pretty similar to "Happy Birthday" in the U.S. Listen:

¡Cumpleaños feliz, deseamos a tí,	*(We wish you a happy birthday)*
Feliz cumpleaños, deseamos a tí!	*(We wish you a happy birthday)*

Do you think you can sing it with me? This time, instead of singing it to "amiguito," let's sing it to Lisa. Okay?

Grandpa, Tony & Lisa:

Feliz, feliz en tu día,	*(Happiness on your day,)*
Lisa, que Dios te bendiga!	*(Lisa, may God bless you!)*
Que reine la paz en tu día,	*(May peace reign on your day,)*
Y que cumplas muchos más!	*(And have many more)*
¡Cumpleaños feliz, deseamos a tí,	*(We wish you a happy birthday)*
Feliz cumpleaños, deseamos a tí!	*(We wish you a happy birthday)*

Grandpa: Good. Let's sing it again. For Tony this time!

Grandpa, Tony & Lisa:

Feliz, feliz en tu día,	*(Happiness on your day,)*
Tony, que Dios te bendiga!	*(Tony, may God bless you!)*
Que reine la paz en tu día,	*(May peace reign on your day,)*
Y que cumplas muchos más!	*(And have many more)*
¡Cumpleaños feliz, deseamos a tí,	*(We wish you a happy birthday)*
Feliz cumpleaños, deseamos a tí!	*(We wish you a happy birthday)*

Grandpa: Good job! And happy birthday!

 Turn the audio off.

Performance Challenge:

Now that you have learned a new song, share your Spanish with a parent, friend, or one of your brothers and sisters by teaching them the song. Remember to teach it in Spanish and then translate the words into English if your partner does not understand Spanish. For an even greater challenge, try writing a song about your culture and put it to the tune of the Spanish song you just learned. If you need an idea to get you started, just think of what a visitor from another country would like to know about you and your family.

De Colores

(Ditties)

  Turn the audio on.

Track 8 **Tony:** So, what might the song be a clue about?

Grandpa: Let me think. Well, now that I think about it, when Bruno and I were working together on research, "Dios te bendiga" was the name of a very famous collection of folk songs. Let's see—where was that book?

Narrator: You follow your grandpa through the stacks of books until he finds what he is looking for.

Grandpa: Here it is. Now what? There must be a hundred songs in this book.

Lisa: But Grandpa, look. There's a piece of paper stuck in this page.

Tony: What is it?

Grandpa: It looks like some sort of clue. There are several complicated words involved. Look at the pages that it's stuck between, though—this is a significant song. It's a song about how beautiful all the colors are. Ever since ancient times, people in Latin America have loved color, in their dress, their homes, and in nature.

Tony: That's true Grandpa. It seems like everything here is painted in beautiful colors.

Lisa: Teach it to us, please?

Tony: Yeah! We need to figure out what Bruno was trying to tell us.

Grandpa: Okay. First, let's go back to the hotel just in case Bruno tries to let us know where to meet him next.

Narrator: Back in your room, Grandpa Glen pulls out his guitar and begins to teach you the song about the colors of spring in the countryside.

Grandpa: Listen carefully. This song is a bit more difficult than the ones you already know.

> De colores, de colores
>
> Se visten los campos en la primavera.
>
> De colores, de colores
>
> Son los pajarillos que vienen de fuera.
>
> De colores, de colores
>
> Es el arco iris que vemos lucir.
>
> Y por eso los grandes amores
>
> De muchos colores me gustan a mí.
>
> Y por eso los grandes amores

De muchos colores me gustan a mí.

Lisa: Wow. That's really pretty.

Grandpa: Yes, it is. Let's sing the first verse together slowly so that you can follow along.

Grandpa, Tony & Lisa:

De colores, de colores

Se visten los campos en la primavera.

De colores, de colores

Son los pajarillos que vienen de fuera.

De colores, de colores

Es el arco iris que vemos lucir.

Y por eso los grandes amores

De muchos colores me gustan a mí.

Y por eso los grandes amores

De muchos colores me gustan a mí.

Grandpa: Good. Now listen to the second verse. It's not very different.

De colores, de colores

Brillantes y finos se viste la aurora.

De colores, de colores

Son los mil reflejos que el sol atesora.

De colores, de colores,

Se viste el diamante que vemos lucir.

Y por eso los grandes amores

De muchos colores me gustan a mí.

Y por eso los grandes amores

De muchos colores me gustan a mí.

Now, let's sing it together.

Grandpa, Tony & Lisa:

>De colores, de colores
>
>Brillantes y finos se viste la aurora.
>
>De colores, de colores
>
>Son los mil reflejos que el sol atesora.
>
>De colores, de colores,
>
>Se viste el diamante que vemos lucir.
>
>Y por eso los grandes amores
>
>De muchos colores me gustan a mí.
>
>Y por eso los grandes amores
>
>De muchos colores me gustan a mí.

Grandpa: Very good. Let's sing the whole thing through one more time.

Grandpa, Tony & Lisa:

>De colores, de colores
>
>Se visten los campos en la primavera.
>
>De colores, de colores
>
>Son los pajarillos que vienen de fuera.
>
>De colores, de colores
>
>Es el arco iris que vemos lucir.
>
>Y por eso los grandes amores
>
>De muchos colores me gustan a mí.
>
>Y por eso los grandes amores
>
>De muchos colores me gustan a mí.

>De colores, de colores
>
>Brillantes y finos se viste la aurora.
>
>De colores, de colores
>
>Son los mil reflejos que el sol atesora.
>
>De colores, de colores,
>
>Se viste el diamante que vemos lucir.

Y por eso los grandes amores

De muchos colores me gustan a mí.

Y por eso los grandes amores

De muchos colores me gustan a mí.

Grandpa: Good job children. That was very nice.

 Turn the audio off.

Performance Challenge:

Now that you have learned a new song, share your Spanish with a parent, friend, or one of your brothers and sisters by teaching them the song. Remember to teach it in Spanish and then translate the words into English if your partner does not understand Spanish. For an even greater challenge, try writing a song about your culture and put it to the tune of the Spanish song you just learned. If you need an idea to get you started, just think of what a visitor from another country would like to know about you and your family.

The Hunter and the Thief

(Match and Learn)

 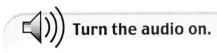 **Turn the audio on.**

Track 9

Tony: So what do you think that song means, Grandpa?

Grandpa: Well, I happen to know that it's a song that is sung at the spring fair every year in Alajuela, a town not too far from here.

Lisa: That must be where Bruno wants to meet us! We should go!

Grandpa: I'm afraid it's too late to go tonight. Let's wait until tomorrow morning.

Tony: But, Grandpa, what if Malo—

Grandpa: No buts, Tony. It's too late to be wandering all over the country. Besides, I think youre going to need all the time you can get to learn the story you'll need to know in order to figure out this riddle. It's one from my folklore research, and it's a little bit difficult.

Narrator: You both look over the riddle, but you don't know any of the words you need to solve it.

Lisa: I don't know theses words, Grandpa. Will you teach us?

Grandpa: Well, let's start out with some of the words that you need to know.

 Practice your new Spanish words by pointing to what you hear. Look at picture box #1 in your workbook.

Track 10

1.

la mujer the woman	*el águila* the eagle
la comida the food	*el ladrón* the thief

2.

la cárcel the prison	*el policía* the police
el águila the eagle	*la comida* the food

3.

el cazador / the hunter	atrapa / traps
roba / robs	arresta / arrests

4.

traga / swallows	el águila y el ladrón / the eagle & the thief
el policía y el cazador / the police & the hunter	la mujer y la comida / the woman & the food

5.

el policía arresta / the police arrest	el águila come / the eagle eats
el ladrón robs / the thief robs	el gato atrapa / the cat traps

6.

la serpiente traga / the snake swallows	el ratón come la comida / the mouse eats the food
el águila cae / the eagle falls	el cazador mata

7.

la ladrón está en la cárcel / the thief is in prison	la mujer prepara la comida / the woman prepares the food
el gato atrapa el ratón / the cat traps the mouse	la serpiente traga el gato / the snake swallows the cat

8.

el águila / theeagle	el cazador mata el águila / the hunter kills the eagle
el ladrón roba el águila / the thief robs the eagle	el policía arresta el ladrón / the police arrest the thief

 Turn the audio off.

Performance Challenge:

Draw a scene from the vocabulary you learned in your Match and Learn exercise. After you draw your picture, describe each part of the scene to a parent, friend, or one of your brothers and sisters. Remember to use as much Spanish as you can to talk about your drawing. For an even greater challenge, use the different words you've learned to create sentences. You can either write the sentences or make picture sentences by drawing your own versions of the pictures from the Match and Learn activity.

The Hunter and the Thief I

(Diglot Weave)

Turn the audio on.

Track 11 **Narrator:** The next morning, you and your grandpa begin to drive to Alajuela. While in the car you look out over the jungle.

Grandpa: So, do you think you learned all of the words well enough last night?

Lisa: I think so.

Grandpa: Good. If Malo's really in Alajuela, we're going to have to hurry. Luckily, I have a friend who lives in Alajuela. We can call her. Her name is Sofía.

Tony: What should we do now?

Grandpa: Well, I think that you're ready to hear the first version of the story. Listen carefully.

Este es mi cuento:

Track 12

Al principio la mujer prepara la comida.

Here is la mujer preparing la comida.

Después de ésto el ratón viene y come la comida.

Here is el ratón eating la comida.

Después de ésto el gato viene y atrapa el ratón.

Here is el gato catching el ratón.

Después de ésto la serpiente viene y traga el gato.

Here is la serpiente swallowing el gato.

Después de ésto el águila viene y cae sobre la serpiente.

Here is el águila falling upon la serpiente.

Después de ésto el cazador viene y mata al águila.

Here is el cazador killing el águila.

Después de ésto el ladrón viene y roba el águila

Here is el ladrón stealing el águila.

Después de ésto el policía viene y arresta el ladrón.

Here is el policía arresting el ladrón.

Y el ladrón va a la cárcel.

Y aquí está el ladrón en la cárcel.

Poor mujer! Poor ratón!

Poor gato! Poor serpiente!

Poor águila! Poor cazador!

Y poor ladrón!

 Turn the audio off.

Performance Challenge:

There are four parts to this Performance Challenge:

1. Read the story silently to yourself.
2. Read the story aloud to yourself.
3. Read the story aloud to a parent, friend or one of your brothers and sisters.
4. Retell the story in your own words, using as much Spanish as you can, to a parent, friend or one of your brothers and sisters. Don't worry if you can't remember every word. Do the best you can, and review the audio if you need to.

For an even greater challenge, write the next chapter for each diglot weave. If the story hadn't ended, what would happen next?

The Hunter and the Thief I

(Review Questions)

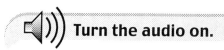 **Turn the audio on.**

Track 13

Narrator: Alajuela is lovely, surrounded by enormous green mountains. It is much smaller than San José, but all of the "Ticos" are just as friendly.

Lisa: It seems like everything here is covered with jungle, Grandpa.

Grandpa: Well, much of it is, Lisa. But there're also several cities and plantations, mostly banana and coffee plantations.

Narrator: Your grandpa takes you out to the outdoor market where he has agreed to meet his friend Sofía.

Tony: Gosh, Grandpa, you know people everywhere.

Grandpa: Well, Tony, I travel a great deal. Don't forget, if you are friendly everywhere you go, you will never have a shortage of friends. I know Sofía from when I was taking a nature tour out here. She's a botanist who studies the plants and animals in the rainforest.

Lisa: Cool. I bet there're a lot to study.

Grandpa: That's very true, Lisa. There're animals in the rainforest who have never even been seen or studied by any scientist.

Narrator: You begin walking around the market. There are many interesting booths and stands for you to explore. You both go over to examine a booth filled with beautiful jade necklaces.

Lisa: Tony! Look—

Tony: What?

Lisa: Never mind. For just a second I was sure I saw Malo in the crowd, but he's gone now.

Tony: Wow. That's kind of scary. Do you really think it was him?

Lisa: I don't know. Part of me wants him to be here—it would mean we were on the right track—but part of me is scared. I don't want him to see me.

Tony: Let's find Grandpa, just in case.

Narrator: You both rejoin your grandpa. He is concerned when you tell him you might have seen Malo, and he begins to look around for Sofía.

Grandpa: I hope that Sofía didn't lose us in the crowd. She should be here by now.

Tony: Don't worry, Grandpa. We're safe as long as we're together.

Grandpa: That's right. Still, you two need to learn that story. I'm going to ask you some review questions to see how much you remember.

True or False

1. *El cazador mata el águila.*

2. *La serpiente traga el ratón.*

3. *El policía arresta el cazador.*

4. *El ladrón va a la cárcel.*

5. *El ratón come la comida.*

 Turn the audio off.

Answers: 1.T 2.F 3.F 4.T 5.T

The Hunter and the Thief II

(Diglot Weave)

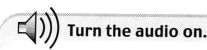 **Turn the audio on.**

Track 15

Narrator: You have just finished answering your grandpa's questions when a slender, middle-aged woman approaches you. She has a friendly, open face and gray streaks in her black hair.

Sofía: ¡Glen! ¡Qué gusto verte!

Grandpa: ¡Sofía! Me da gusto verte. Déjame presentar a mis nietos. This is Tony, and this is Lisa.

Tony: ¿Como está?

Lisa: Mucho gusto.

Grandpa: Children, this is my friend Sofía.

Narrator: Sofía invites you to go to a restaurant with her for lunch. You all sit outside a cafe while Grandpa tells Sofía about the situation. Sofía orders a special dessert for you called flan. It is a tasty custard with caramel sauce. If you would like to try and make flan, there is a recipe in the back of your workbook. Of course, no sooner has Sofía heard the entire story from Grandpa than she offers her help in tracking down Malo and Bruno. She asks to see the clues and puzzles that you have collected so far. You begin walking back to the hotel together.

Grandpa: Sofía doesn't know the story that we're learning, so I'm going to tell all of you the second version.

Ahora we're going to see qué tan bien you learned el cuento.

¿Qué pasó primero?

Track 16

La mujer preparó la comida.

Aquí está la mujer preparando la comida.

¿Qué pasó después de éso?

Después de éso un ratón vino y comió la comida.

Aquí está el ratón comiendo la comida.

¿Qué pasó después de éso?

Después de éso el gato vino y atrapó el ratón.

Aquí está el gato atrapando el ratón.

¿Qué pasó despúes de éso?
Después de éso la serpiente vino y tragó el gato.
Aquí está la serpiente tragando el gato.

¿Qué pasó despúes de éso?
Después de éso el águila vino y cayó sobre la serpiente.
Aquí está el águila cayendo sobre la serpiente.

¿Qué pasó despúes de éso?
Después de éso el cazador vino y mató el águila.
Aquí está el cazador matando el águila.

¿Qué pasó despúes de éso?
Después de éso el ladrón vino y robó el águila.
Aquí está el ladrón robando el águila.

¿Qué pasó despúes de éso?
Después de éso el policía vino y arrestó el ladrón.
Aquí está el policía arrestando el ladrón.

¿Qué pasó despúes de éso?
El ladrón fue a la cárcel.
Y aquí está el ladrón en la cárcel.

 Turn the audio off.

Performance Challenge:

There are four parts to this Performance Challenge:
1. Read the story silently to yourself.
2. Read the story aloud to yourself.
3. Read the story aloud to a parent, friend or one of your brothers and sisters.
4. Retell the story in your own words, using as much Spanish as you can, to a parent, friend or one of your brothers and sisters. Don't worry if you can't remember every word. Do the best you can, and review the audio if you need to.
For an even greater challenge, write the next chapter for each diglot weave. If the story hadn't ended, what would happen next?

The Hunter and the Thief II

(Story Telling)

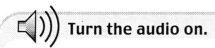 **Turn the audio on.**

Track 17

Sofía: ¿ No es demasiado peligroso para los niños?

Grandpa: Dangerous? Yes, it is a little. The children have been a great help so far, though. They're learning more and more Spanish.

Sofía: ¿Qué tanto entienden?

Grandpa: They are learning more and more every day. They've been learning many new words in order to understand the next story.

Sofía: ¿De veras? Me gustaría escuchar lo que han aprendido.

Grandpa: What do you say, children? Do you want to show your Spanish off for Sofía?

Tony: Sure.

Lisa: Okay.

Grandpa: Great. Let's show her how much of the story you understood. I want you to tell the story back to us. Use as much Spanish as you can!

 Turn the audio off.

Now retell the story, using as much Spanish as you can.

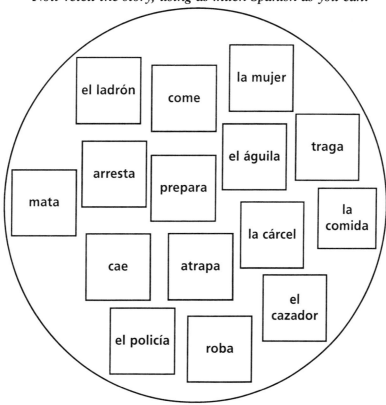

Word Puzzle 3

(Story Telling)

  Turn the audio on.

Track 18 **Narrator:** You arrive at the hotel and take out the puzzle that Bruno left for you.

Lisa: We should try to solve it now.

Tony: Of course. The sooner we solve the puzzle, the sooner we can find out where Bruno wants to meet us.

Lisa: Yeah. And we want to get that statue from Malo before he takes it wherever he's taking it.

Grandpa: Well, I have a suspicion about that.

Tony: Really? What?

Grandpa: I wasn't sure why Malo would be risking so much just to steal the treasure. I've decided that he is probably working for someone who is collecting Mayan artifacts. It would have to be someone very rich, someone who was willing to pay a great deal of money for the statue. If Malo sells the statue, then our chances of ever recovering it are almost impossible.

Lisa: But that's awful! Do you think that we'll have time to find it before he sells it?

Grandpa: I'm not sure. You see, the buyer is probably right here in Costa Rica. I can't think of any other reason why Malo would come here.

Sofía: Te ayudaré con el problema si puedo.

Grandpa: Thank you, Sofía. We might need your help. You know the area much better than we do.

Tony: Yeah. Let's take a look.

 Turn the audio off.

Fill in the blanks in the puzzle below by following the numbered clues. The letters that fall in the circled blanks will make additional words that will help you on your adventure.

1. **Food**

2. **Eagle**

3. **Police**

4. **Mouse**

5. **Thief**

6. **Snake**

7. **Cat**

8. **Hunter**

9. **He arrests**

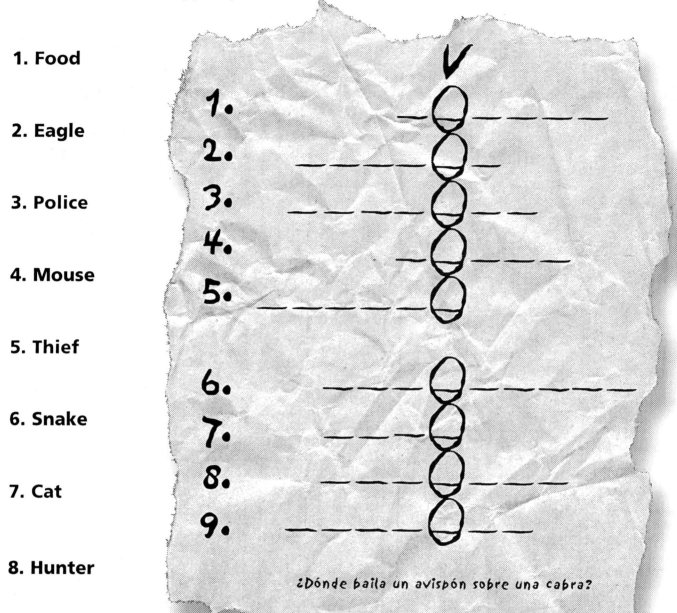

¿Dónde baila un avispón sobre una cabra?

A Boy and His Goat

(Scatter Chart)

  Turn the audio on.

Track 19

Grandpa: Look here. There's a riddle on the bottom of the page as well. It says, "¿Dónde baila un avispón sobre una cabra?" That sounds like a hard riddle. Besides, what does the word "Poas" mean?

Sofía: ¡Poas! ¡Claro!

Lisa: What is it, Sofía?

Sofía: Poas es el volcán activo cerca de aquí.

Grandpa: An active volcano? That sounds dangerous.

Tony: We're going to see an active volcano? Cool!

Grandpa: I'm not sure that's such a good idea. Maybe you two better stay home for this. It doesn't sound very safe.

Lisa: Oh, please, Grandpa? We promise that we'll be a big help.

Tony: Yeah! Besides, we might never get a chance to see a volcano again!

Grandpa: Well . . . you two have both been very good about learning the story . . . I wouldn't have been able to do the puzzle without you . . . okay. I'd better start to teach you the story that would answer the riddle, then. We'll start with the new words.

Look at the pictures on your workbook page and point to what you hear..

Track 20

le lechuga
the lettuce

el vecino
the neighbor

el jardín
the garden

el conejo
the rabbit

los vegetales
the vegetables

la cabra
the goat

mira
looks

pequeño
small

el cerco
the fence

 Turn the audio off.

Performance Challenge:

There are four parts to this Performance Challenge:

1. Read the story silently to yourself.
2. Read the story aloud to yourself.
3. Read the story aloud to a parent, friend or one of your brothers and sisters.
4. Retell the story in your own words, using as much Spanish as you can, to a parent, friend or one of your brothers and sisters.

Don't worry if you can't remember every word. Do the best you can, and review the audio if you need to.

For an even greater challenge, write the next chapter for each diglot weave. If the story hadn't ended, what would happen next?

A Boy and His Goat I

(Diglot Weave)

  Turn the audio on.

Track 21 **Narrator:** It is very early the next morning when you begin climbing up Poas with Sofía as your guide. You are very lucky to have her there. She points out all the local plants and animals to you. Perhaps most stunning is the brilliant red and emerald "quetzal," a magnificent bird perched on a branch near the trail.

Lisa: All of the trees and plants seem so little up here.

Grandpa: That's right, Lisa. Up in the mountains like this, because of the altitude, nothing grows very large. They call it a "cloud forest."

Tony: Wow! How far are we from the top?

Grandpa: Another half hour or so. Do you remember the words I taught you last night? Well, then, I think you're ready to hear the story. It's called "A Boy and His Goat."

 ## Un niño y su cabra

Track 22 *Había una vez un niño que se llamaba Pablo. El had a goat que fancied el jardín del vecino.*

Each día Pablo went con su cabra a un pasture cerca de la casa de su vecino. There la cabra ate la sweet grass.

Y each day, as they pasaba la casa del vecino la cabra looked longingly al jardín de vegetales.

Several veces he tried to break down el fence so he could entrar al jardín y comer los vegetales. La lettuce seemed especialmente deliciosa.

Un día as Pablo led su cabra al pasto, they were pasando el jardín, y la cabra butted el cerco con sus horns y broke it.

Immediately la cabra corrió y began a comer la lechuga deliciosa.

Pablo tugged en la rope with all su fuerza. Él shouted y whistled, pero la cabra didn't pay attention . . . no le hizo caso. He wouldn't even lift la cabeza. He just kept on comiendo las hojas de lechuga.

Con toda su fuerza Pablo tried to remove la cabra del jardín pero he couldn't.

So se sentó y began a llorar.

By chance, en ese momento, un pequeño rabbit pasó.

"Hola, niño. ¿Why lloras?"

"Estoy llorando porque my cabra rompió el cerco del vecino. Ahora está comiendo los vegetales, y yo no puedo get him out. I can't even get him to raise la cabeza."

"Well éso shouldn't be so difícil; I'll do it."

El conejo saltó a la cabra y gritó, "¡Eh, Cabra, look a mí!"

El conejo flopped las orejas y saltó y saltó gritando, "¡Eh, tuuuuú! ¡Eh tú! mírame a mí."

But la cabra didn't pay any attention. . .no le hizo caso. He wouldn't even levantar la cabeza, instead he kept on comiendo la lechuga.

Finally el conejo gave up y se sentó at Pablo's side, y he began a llorar.

En ese momento pasó una zorra muy proudly, lifting la cola high so that everyone could admire it.

"Eh, Conejo ¿por qué estás llorando?

"Estoy llorando porque la cabra didn't pay attention to me, y el niño está llorando porque su cabra rompió el cerco del vecino y está comiendo el jardín, y él can't get su cabra to come out."

"Bueno," dijo Señora Zorra, "No veo any problema aquí. So, if you don't mind, yo will do it."

Then Señora Zorra corrió a la cabra and began to walk en frente de la cabra. All the time diciendo, "Eh, Cabra, mírame a mí."

But la cabra no le hizo caso. He wouldn't even levantar la cabeza. He just kept comiendo la lechuga.

Finally Señora Zorra gave up y se sentó y began a llorar beside el conejo.

En ese momento un lobo grande y prideful pasó.

"Señora Zorra ¿por qué estás llorando? Y ¿por qué están llorando todos?"

"Yo estoy llorando por the same razón que el conejo, y el conejo está llorando por la same razón que el niño.

"Y ¿por qué está llorando el niño?"

"El niño está llorando porque su cabra rompió el cerco del vecino y está comiendo la lechuga. Y ahora no puede remove la cabra.

"Bueno, no veo ningún problema aquí. Yo puedo hacerlo."

El lobo grande went al jardín y gruñó a la cabra, "Grrrrr," and made faces a la cabra y even sopló y fopló.

But la cabra no le hizo caso, ni siquiera levantaba la cabeza. He just siguió comiendo la lechuga.

So el lobo grande se sentó y se puso a llorar.

En ese momento pasó un hornet.

"Lobo, ¿por qué lloras?"

"Bueno, estoy llorando por la misma razón que la zorra, y la zorra está llorando por la misma razón que el conejo, y el conejo está llorando por la misma razón que el niño."

"Y ¿por qué está llorando el niño?"

"El niño está llorando porque su cabra rompió el cerco del vecino y está comiendo la lechuga. Now he can't get la cabra to come out, ni le puede hacer levanta la cabeza."

"Pues yo no veo ningún problema aquí. Yo puedo hacerlo," dijo el hornet. "Yo can remove la cabra del jardín."

En un momento they all stopped llorando. ¿Un hornet so pequeño was going to remove la cabra del jardín? ¿Cómo could it be?

Todos watched while el avispón flew over to la cabra. Y flew cerca de las orejas de la cabra y finally he landed en su nariz.

Then el avispón se puso to dance en la nariz de la cabra y éso tickled la nariz de la cabra, y la cabra began to laugh,"jii, jii. . .jaa, jaa," until he realized what estaba tickling su nariz.

"UN AVISPÓN!" La cabra saltó en el aire y el avispón stung him en la nariz y la cabra left el jardín corriendo.

El avispón flew away, el lobo slunk down el camino, la zorra corrió por el pasto, y el conejo saltó, y éste es el fin.

 Turn the audio off.

Performance Challenge:

There are four parts to this Performance Challenge:
1. Read the story silently to yourself.
2. Read the story aloud to yourself.
3. Read the story aloud to a parent, friend or one of your brothers and sisters.
4. Retell the story in your own words, using as much Spanish as you can, to a parent, friend or one of your brothers and sisters. Don't worry if you can't remember every word. Do the best you can, and review the audio if you need to.

For an even greater challenge, write the next chapter for each diglot weave. If the story hadn't ended, what would happen next?

A Boy and His Goat

(Review Questions)

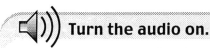 **Turn the audio on.**

Track 23

Narrator: The sun is high in the sky by the time you get near the top of the volcano. It is a large crater, which looks down on a lake that steams and boils. Sofía explains that the magma--the hot, melted rock deep inside the volcano, heats the lake, but no longer explodes. It is a most incredible sight.

Tony: Wow. It looks like it could erupt at any second.

Grandpa: Actually, Tony, it erupted a long time ago. Now, there's no real danger. Just don't fall in.

Lisa: But the crater is huge! How will we ever find the clue?

Tony: We probably need to solve the riddle first. What was it? "Dónde baila un avispón sobre una cabra?"

Grandpa: You're right, and we're running out of time. Let's see how much of the story you remember.

True or False.

1. *Todos los días Pablo walks with su cabra al pasto and past el jardín del vecino.*

2. *Pablo doesn't try to keep su cabra out of el jardín.*

3. *El conejo shakes la cola de la cabra to get the attention de la cabra.*

4. *El lobo is hungry and wants to comer el conejo.*

5. *Al fin el avispón stung la cabra en la nariz.*

Track 24

 Turn the audio off.

Answers: 1.T 2.F 3.F 4.F 5.T

A Boy and His Goat II

(Diglot Weave)

  Turn the audio on.

Track 25 **Grandpa:** Well, it looks like you're learning the story pretty well, but we haven't figured out the riddle yet. I suggest we split up and see what we will find.

Sofía: Bueno. Yo voy a ver aquí a la derecha.

Grandpa: Good. I'll search to the left. You two look over this area here, and make sure you stay together. Okay?

Narrator: You agree, even though it makes you nervous to be standing so close to the steaming hot lake.

Lisa: It looks kind of spooky, doesn't it?

Tony: Yeah. Some of the rocks even look like faces, like they're watching us.

Narrator: Just then, you hear footsteps approaching.

Tony: Do you hear that?

Lisa: Don't worry. It's probably Grandpa Glen coming back.

Tony: What if it isn't?

Narrator: You look at each other for a moment, then run and hide behind some trees. Peering through the green leaves, you can see two men heading down the mountain.

Malo: No sé por qué nos hiciste venir aquí. Estamos perdiendo tiempo.

Lisa: It's Malo and Bruno!

Narrator: You wait until they have disappeared down the mountain, then you both run over to your grandpa as fast as you can and tell him what happened.

Grandpa: Well, it looks like we just missed them again. At least we know where they were, though. Let's go back to where you saw them. The clue would be close.

Narrator: You carefully make your way back to the lake.

Grandpa: Okay. Before we begin, I think that you're ready to hear the more advanced version of the story. Listen carefully, and try to find anything that has to do with the clue.

 ## Un niño y su cabra

Track 26 *Había una vez un niño que se llamaba Pablo. El tenía una cabra al que le gustaba el jardín del vecino.*

Cada día Pablo caminaba con su cabra a un pasto cerca de la casa de su vecino. Allí la cabra comía la hierba.

Y cada día, al pasar la casa del vecino la cabra veía el jardín de vegetales con anhelo.

Varias veces la cabra intentaba romper el cerco para entrar y comer los vegetales. La lechuga le parecía especialmente deliciosa.

Un día, mientras Pablo caminaba al pasto con su cabra, pasó el jardín, y la cabra rompió el cerco con los cuernos.

Inmediatemente corrió y se puso a comer la lechuga.

Pablo jaló en la cuerda con toda su fuerza. Él gritaba y chiflaba, pero la cabra no le hizo caso, ni levantó la cabeza. Solo siguió comiendo las hojas de la lechuga.

Con toda su fuerza Pablo intentó a sacar la cabra del jardín pero no pudo.

Así que se sentó y se puso a llorar.

Por casualidad, en ese momento, un pequeño conejo pasó.

"Hola niño. ¿Por qué lloras?"

"Estoy llorando porque mi cabra rompió el cerco de mi vecino y ahora está comiendo los vegetales, y yo no puedo sacarlo, ni le puedo hacer se levanta la cabeza."

"Bueno éso no debe ser tan difícil. Yo puedo hacerlo."

El conejo saltó a la cabra y gritó: "¡Eh, Cabra, mírame a mí!"

El conejo le hacía señas con las orejas y saltaba y saltaba gritando "¡Eh tuuuuú! ¡Eh tú! mírame a mí.

Pero la cabra no le hizo caso, ni levantó la cabeza, sino siguió comiendo la lechuga.

Por fin el conejo dejó de intentar y se sentó a lado de Pablo, y se puso a llorar.

En ese momento pasó una zorra muy orgullosa, llevando la cola alta para que todos pudieran verla."Eh, Conejo ¿por qué están llorando?"

"Estoy llorando porque la cabra no me hizo caso, y el niño está llorando porque su cabra rompió el cerco del vecino y está comiendo el jardín, y él no lo puede sacar."

"Bueno," dijo Señora Zorra, "No veo ningún problema aquí. Así que, si les parece bien, yo puedo hacerlo.

Entonces Señora Zorra corrió a la cabra y se puso a caminar enfrente de la cabra. Todo el tiempo diciendo, "Eh, Cabra, mírame a mí."

Pero la cabra no le hizo caso, ni levantó la cabeza, sino siguió comiendo la lechuga.

Por fin Señora Zorra dejó de intentar y se sentó y se puso a llorar a lado del conejo.

En ese momento un lobo grande y orgulloso pasó.

"Señora Zorra ¿por qué estás llorando? Y por qué están llorando todos?"

"*Yo estoy llorando por la misma razón que el conejo, y el conejo está llorando por la misma razón que el niño.*"

"*Y ¿por qué está llorando el niño?*"

"*El niño está llorando porque su cabra rompió el cerco del vecino y está comiendo la lechuga. Y ahora no puede sacar la cabra, y ni le puede hacer se levanta la cabeza.*

Bueno, no veo ningún problema aquí. Yo lo haré.

El lobo grande se fue al jardín y gruño a la cabra, "Grrrrr," hacía caras a la cabra y hasta sopló y fopló.

Pero la cabra no le hizo caso, ni levantó la cabeza, sino siguió comiendo la lechuga.

Así que el lobo se sentó y se puso a llorar.

En ese momento pasó un avispón.

"*Lobo ¿por qué lloras?*"

"*Bueno, estoy llorando por la misma razón que la zorra, y la zorra está llorando por la misma razón que el conejo, y el conejo está llorando por la misma razón que el niño.*"

"*Y ¿por qué está llorando el niño?*"

"*El niño está llorando porque su cabra rompió el cerco del vecino y está comiendo la lechuga. Ahora no puede sacarlo y ni le puede hacer se levanta la cabeza.*"

"*Pues yo no veo ningún problema aquí. Yo puedo hacer éso,*" dijo el avispón, "*yo puedo sacar la cabra del jardín.*"

En un momento todos dejaron de llorar. "¿Un avispón tan chiquita va a sacar la cabra del jardín? ¿Como podría ser?"

Todos vieron mientras el avispón voló sobre la cabra. Volaba y volaba cerca de las orejas de la cabra y por fin aterrizó en su nariz.

Entonces el avispón se puso a bailar en la nariz de la cabra y eso le hacía cosquillas, y la cabra se reía, "jii, jii. . .jaa, jaa," hasta que se dió cuenta de lo que era que le estaba dando cosquillas.

"*UN AVISPÓN!*" *La cabra saltó en el aire y el avispón le picó en la nariz y la cabra se fue corriendo del jardín.*

El avispón se fue volando, el lobo se escurrió por el camino, la zorra se fue corriendo por el pasto, el conejo se fue saltando, y éste es el fin.

 Turn the audio off.

Performance Challenge:

There are four parts to this Performance Challenge:

1. Read the story silently to yourself.
2. Read the story aloud to yourself.
3. Read the story aloud to a parent, friend or one of your brothers and sisters.
4. Retell the story in your own words, using as much Spanish as you can, to a parent, friend or one of your brothers and sisters.

Don't worry if you can't remember every word. Do the best you can, and review the audio if you need to.

For an even greater challenge, write the next chapter for each diglot weave. If the story hadn't ended, what would happen next?

A Boy and His Goat II

(Story Telling)

  Turn the audio on.

Narrator: Sofía comes and joins you. You fill her in on all that has happened. She reminds you that you are running out of time.

Grandpa: You're right, Sofía. We need to solve the clue.

Lisa: Okay. Let's think this through. What was the clue again?

Grandpa: "¿Dónde baila un avispón sobre una cabra?"

Tony: We know the "avispón" did a "baile" on the "cabra" . . .

Lisa: On his "nariz"!

Grandpa: Of course! The answer to the riddle must be "nose."

Tony: But how does that help us find the next clue?

Lisa: I know! It's like you said, Tony. The rocks here look like huge faces. See that one over there?

Tony: Yeah! And that outcropping of rock would be the "nariz"!

Grandpa: Good job, children!

Sofía: ¡Bien hecho!

Narrator: You all get close to the rock, which is dangerously near the boiling water. By holding hands, you manage to stretch across and feel on top of the rock.

Tony: We've got it!

Grandpa: Let me see . . . yes! It's another puzzle. It looks hard.

Lisa: Do you think that we can do it?

Grandpa: I think so. Let's review the story first, for the words we need. Why don't you two tell it back to Sofía and me in Spanish?

 Turn the audio off.

Now retell the story using as much Spanish as you can.

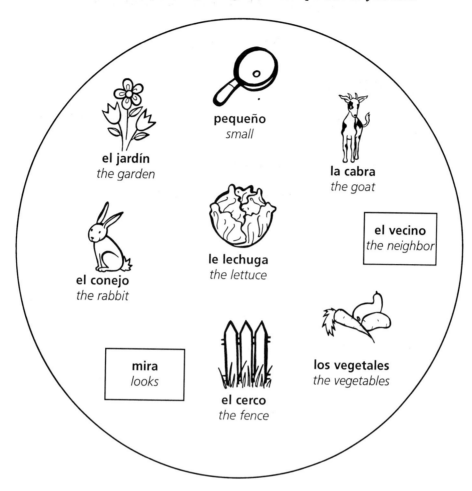

Word Puzzle 4

(A Boy and His Goat)

Turn the audio on.

Narrator: You all begin the slow hike down the mountain as you look over the puzzle. The sun in getting low, and you're anxious to get home before dark.

Sofía: Parece que conocen el cuento bastante bien.

Grandpa: Yes, they're learning quickly. We still need to figure out that clue, though, so that we can follow Malo and Bruno.

Tony: You're right. Let's look it over and see if we can figure it out.

 ## Turn the audio off.

Fill in the blanks in the puzzle below by following the numbered clues. The letters that fall in the circled blanks will make additional words that will help you on your adventure.

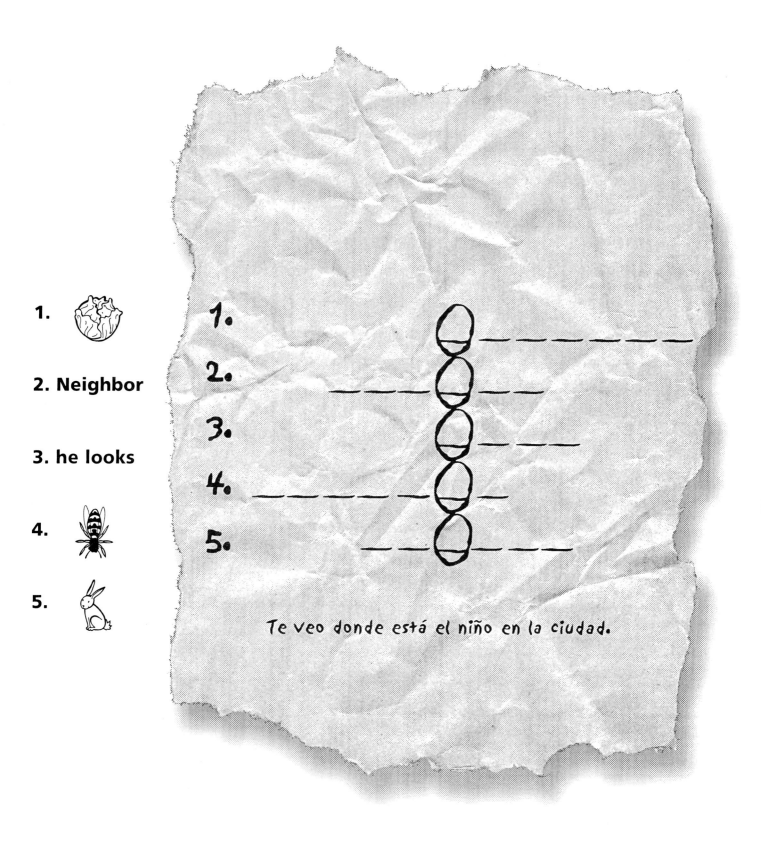

1.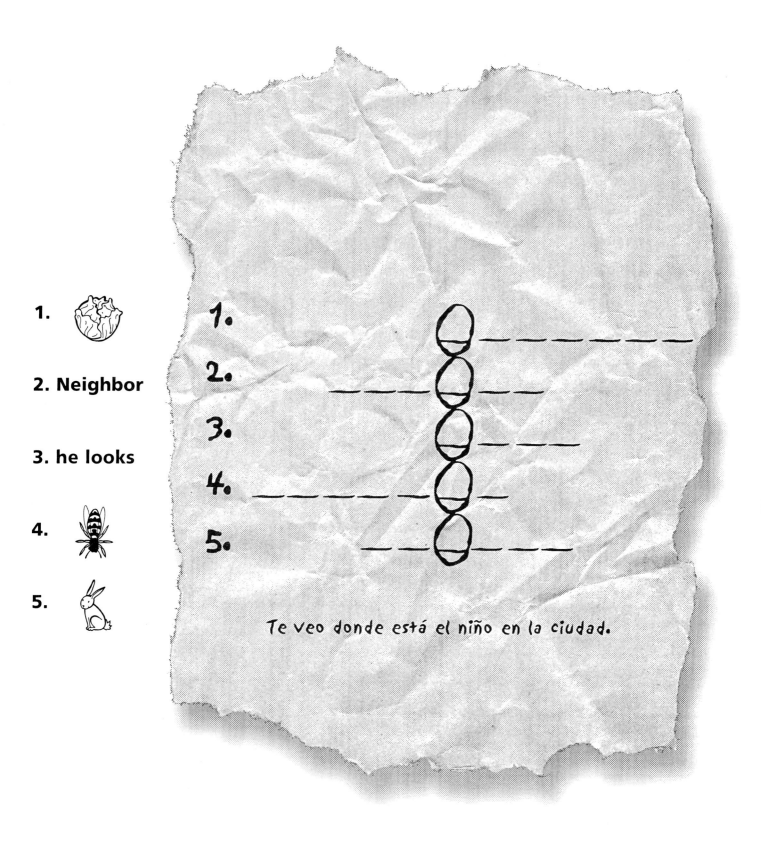

2. **Neighbor**

3. **he looks**

4.

5.

Te veo donde está el niño en la ciudad.

A Sandwich in the Universe

(Horseshoe Story)

  Turn the audio on.

Track 29 **Grandpa:** The puzzle says "Limón." I know where that is.

Sofía: Debemos ir para allá, rápido.

Grandpa: You're right. If we leave right away, we should get there just before dark.

Tony: What does this mean at the bottom of the puzzle? It looks like another riddle. It says, "Te veo donde está el niño en la ciudad." I don't know most of those words.

Grandpa: That's okay. I can teach you a story that will help you figure it out. For right now, though, we need to get going. Thank you for your help, Sofía. We couldn't have done it without you.

Sofía: De nada.

Narrator: After saying goodbye to Sofía, you all get in the car and begin to drive to Limón.

Lisa: Can you tell us the story now, Grandpa, so that we can figure out the riddle?

Grandpa: Of course. It is called, "Un sandwich en el universo."

Un sandwich en el universo

Track 30

Este es un sandwich.
Este es el universo.
En el universo hay una galaxia.
En la galaxia hay una estrella.
Cerca de la estrella hay un planeta se llama Tierra.
En la tierra hay un continente.
En el continente hay un país.
En el país hay una ciudad.
En la ciudad hay un parque.
En el parque hay un niño.
En la mano del niño hay un sandwich.

Un sandwich en la mano de un niño, El niño en el parque,
El parque en la ciudad,
La ciudad en el país,
El país en el continente,
El continente en el planeta que se llama Tierra,
La tierra cerca de la estrella,
La estrella en la galaxia,
La galaxia en el universo.
Y aquí está el sandwich en la mano del niño.

 Turn the audio off.

Performance Challenge:

Create hand actions to represent the actions in the horseshoe story. (For example: Make up different actions to represent the animals you heard about in the story.) After you have created the actions, perform your mini-play for a parent, friend, or one of your bothers and sisters. Remember to narrate your actions in Spanish and then translate your words if your audience does not understand Spanish. For an even greater challenge, try writing your own horseshoe story. Choose several things or people that are related to each other in some way. Think of a chain of events that connects the characters in the story. To finish the story, figure out how the events could be reversed in order to back through the pictures and the plot.

A Sandwich in the Universe

(Scatter Chart)

Track 31

Narrator: You arrive at Limón late at night, and the next morning the three of you wake up and begin your search. The smell of seawater is everywhere, and the port is full of ships loading coffee beans, bananas, and coconuts. As you walk beside the docks, you both run ahead while your grandpa falls behind.

Lisa: Hey, Tony, let's see if we can race to the boat over there. Ready? One, two—

Malo: No, Bruno, hemos perdido demasiado tiempo. ¡Vamos! Tenemos que irnos.

Tony: Lisa! Did you hear that?

Lisa: Yeah! It was Malo. Quick, let's see if we can follow him.

Narrator: You crane your necks around looking for Malo, but can't see over the press of sailors and locals all around. Your grandpa catches up, and you tell him what happened.

Grandpa: Well, if they were here, they've gone now. We'll have to figure out where.

Tony: Okay, Grandpa, where should we go?

Grandpa: I think that we'll have to figure out the riddle to find out.

Lisa: There are still some words I don't understand.

Grandpa: That's okay. Let's go through them and see if we can figure it out.

Look at the pictures on your workbook page and point to what you hear.

la galaxia
the galaxy

el sandwich
the sandwich

la tierra
the earth

el parque
the park

el país
the country

el continente
the continent

el niño
the child

la ciudad
the city

la mano
the hand

la estrella
the star

Turn the audio off.

Performance Challenge:

Choose five of the new words and pictures that you learned in the Scatter Chart. Show the pictures to a parent, friend, or one of your brothers and sisters and explain to them how you think the picture represents the words you have learned. For an even greater challenge, create your own story using the pictures. Bring out the artist in yourself by drawing your own versions of the pictographs and making a book with the story you create.

A Sandwich in the Universe

(Story Telling)

 Turn the audio on.

Track 33

Grandpa: Good job, children. Remember, the riddle is "Te veo donde está el niño en la ciudad." We just need to figure out what that means, and then where in town we should go. Come on, there's a city information booth a couple of streets over.

Narrator: You all leave the docks and go into town until you find the bureau. There is an entire wall filled with brochures and pamphlets for attractions all over town.

Lisa: Wow. There are a lot of places we could meet.

Tony: Yeah. The trick is finding out which place Bruno meant for us to go.

Grandpa: The answer must be in the riddle. Do you remember the story well enough to figure out the clue? Why don't you repeat the story back to me in Spanish?

 Turn the audio off.

Now retell the story using as much Spanish as you can.

Final Word Puzzle

(A Sandwich in the Universe)

  Turn the audio on.

Tony: Okay. In order to solve the riddle, we need to know "Te veo donde está el niño en la ciudad." Right?

Lisa: Right. Now, we know where the "niño" is.

Tony: Yes, in the "parque."

Lisa: Yes, and the "parque" is in the "ciudad."

Grandpa: You're right! The answer must be "parque." Which "parque" do you think that he meant?

Tony: Look, Grandpa. There's a pamphlet here for something called "El Parque Mariposa."

Grandpa: Yes, of course. I've heard of those. Let's take the map and see if we can find it.

Narrator: A half hour later you are standing outside an enormous green house.

Lisa: This doesn't look like a "parque."

Grandpa: Well, Lisa, this is a "parque" where they raise "mariposas". . . butterflies. Let's go inside.

Narrator: Inside the Parque Mariposa, the air is full of flitting butterflies. They scatter away when you walk close to them, but after a moment of standing still they become braver and begin to land on your hands and arms.

Lisa: They're so beautiful.

Grandpa: Be careful not to touch them with your hands, it would hurt their wings. Now, carefully, let's see if we can go find Bruno.

Narrator: Being very quiet, you all begin to wander through the rooms of the green house. Each room is different, filled with butterflies, trees, flowers, and sometimes statues and waterfalls. You are passing by a small waterfall when you see something on the ground.

Tony: Hey, do you see that? It looks like another clue. Grandpa! Come look at this!

Grandpa: Well, it looks like we missed Bruno again, but at least he left us a clue. Let's look at it. Hmm. This looks difficult. We'd better sit down and do it together.

Narrator: You all sit down on a bench, surrounded by butterflies, and begin to look over the puzzle.

 Turn the audio off.

Answer the questions below with the Spanish words. When you have the answer written in Spanish, take the first letter of each answer and cross out the corresponding letter in the letter puzzle below working from left to right.. Place the remaining letters in the blanks provided below, the letters will spell out a clue as to the where-abouts of the stolen artifacts.

What place does Pablo's goat break into to eat the lettuce? _____

Which animal first tries to get Pablo's goat to stop eating the lettuce? _____

What does little brother accidentally cut himself with? _____

Where are the stars? _____

Which animal is very proud about her tail? _____

Which room does Goldilocks fall asleep in? _____

What kind of animal is Pablo's pet? _____

What room does the mouse live in? _____

What does the mouse do in the kitchen after everyone else is asleep? _____

LJACCRABDMGZCOCN

~ ~ ~ ~ ~ ~ ~ ~ ~ ~ ~

Safe Return

(Mission Accomplished)

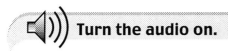 **Turn the audio on.**

Track 35

Tony: "La Ramón." What do you think it means, Grandpa?

Grandpa: I seem to remember a large banana plantation not far outside of town here that has that name. It's owned by a rich, eccentric man.

Lisa: Grandpa, that's it! That must be the man that Malo is selling the statue to!

Tony: And if that's true, then we would have to get there now.

Narrator: Nervous, you all get in the car and drive toward the plantation. The sun is going down just as you arrive.

Lisa: What now, Grandpa?

Grandpa: I'm not sure. Malo was definitely here before us if this is where he was selling the statue. I think the only thing we can do at this point is go to the door. Whoever the man is, we're just going to have to reason with him.

Narrator: You carefully walk behind your grandfather as he approaches and knocks on the door of the mansion. A small, cheerful older man opens the door.

Ramón: ¿Sí? ¿Te puedo ayudar?

Narrator: Slowly, your grandfather begins to tell his story, starting at the beginning. When he starts telling about the statue, the man who answered the door invites you in.

Ramón: Creo que deben venir conmigo.

Grandpa: He wants us to follow him. Stay close, children.

Narrator: The man, Ramón, leads you down a long hall and shows you into a large living room. There, above the mantelpiece, is the statue.

Grandpa: That's it. That's the statue!

Narrator: Your grandfather and Ramón, have a long conversation. Luckily for you, the man is an avid collector of Mayan folklore, but he is mostly interested in conservation. He had no idea that the statue was stolen. He agrees immediately to return it to the museum.

Grandpa: Well, children, this worked out pretty well. We were very lucky. Ramón says that he knows where Malo is staying in Limón, and the police are on their way over now. The statue is safe, Malo will be punished, and I have you two to thank. I could never have done it without you.

Narrator: That night your parents fly in from Progreso. They are so proud of you, and Grandpa Glen can't stop bragging about what a good job you did and how much Spanish you learned. Your parents are impressed, and ask if they can hear your Spanish. You agree, happy with all that you have done and learned.

 Turn the audio off.

Test 2

(Review)

  Turn the audio on.

A. Frame Identifications

For each question, you will see a box with pictures. You will hear a statement about one of the pictures. There will be a pause of 10 seconds to identify the picture, and then the statement will be repeated.

1.

2.

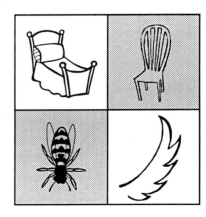

3.

the eagle	the woman
the thief	the food

4.

the police	the eagle
the thief	the hunter

5.

Comprehension Multiple-Choice

Complete the following conversations by choosing the correct answer from the options listed.

1. "¡Sofía! Me da gusto verte. Déjame presentar a mis nietos."

   A. Mucho gusto.

   B. ¡Bien hecho!

   C. Vamos aquí.

   D. De nada.

2. Who owned el jardín con lechuga?

   A. el niño

   B. la cabra

   C. el vecino

   D. la zorra

3. ¿Qué pasó primero?

   A. El gato vino y atrapó el raton.

   B. La mujer preparó comida.

   C. El cazador vino y cayó sobre la serpiente.

   D. El policía vino y arrestó el ladrón.

4. ¿Dónde está la galaxia?

   A. en el parque

   B. en la ciudad

   C. en el país

   D. en el universo

5. ¿Porqué lloras?

   A. Bien hecho! Estoy comiendo la comida.

   B. Mucho gusto. ¿Sabe usted dónde se encuentra uno de éstos?

   C. La cabra rompió el cerco de vecino y está comiendo la lechuga.

   D. Bueno, no veo ningún problema aquí.

Now go on to complete the reading/writing portion of this test.

 Turn the audio off.

Matching

Choose the statements that match and draw a line to connect the two.

1. lettuce

2. fence

3. garden

4. continent

5. eagle

A. jardín

B. continente

C. lechuga

D. águila

E. cerco

True or False

Write T or F for each statement.

_____ 1. El ladrón arrests el policía y puts him in la cárcel.

_____ 2. La cabra en el cuento is afraid of un avispón.

_____ 3. El vecino has lechuga en su jardín.

_____ 4. El cazador eats el águila.

_____ 5. When none of the otros animales knew what to do, el avispón saved the day.

Answer Key

1.

2.

3.

the eagle	the woman
the thief	the food

4.

the police	the eagle
the thief	the hunter

5.

Comprehension Multiple-Choice

1. A. Mucho gusto.

2. C. el vecino

3. B. La mujer preparó comida.

4. D. en el universo

5. C. La cabra rompió el cerco de vecino y está comiendo la lechuga.

Matching

1. C

2. E

3. A

4. B

5. D

True or False

1. F

2. T

3. T

4. F

5. T

Recipes

FLAN

Preheat oven to 325 degrees.

Mix: 3/4 cup sugar

1/3 cup water

Bring to a boil over medium heat. Do not stir, but scrape the sides of the pan to prevent crystallization. Remove from heat when caramelized and turns a light golden brown. Quickly pour in the bottom of a 8 x 10 inch pan.

In a large bowl, beat:

6 eggs

Add: 3/4 cup sugar

1 quart (4 cups) whole milk

1 1/2 tsp vanilla extract

1 tsp lemon juice

Mix well. Pour into pan on the top of caramel mixture. Bake at least 1 hour, until knife inserted in the middle comes out clean.

GUACAMOLE

4 large avocados, very ripe

Garlic salt

1 cup white onion, minced

4 chiles serranos, minced (seeds removed)

1/2 cup cilantro

juice of 1 lime

Mash the avocados in a bowl. Add garlic salt to taste. Add onion, chile, and cilantro. Mix well. May be eaten immediately or refrigerated overnight. Serve with tortilla chips.

SALSA

6-8 Large Tomatoes, very ripe

1 Large Purple Onion

1 Bunch Cilantro

Juice of 1 Lime

Garlic Salt (to taste)

Chili Powder (to taste)

Chop tomatoes into chunks. Chop onion very finely. Tear leaves of cilantro and add to mixture. Squeeze in lime juice and add Garlic Salt and Chili Powder to taste. Beat if refrigerated overnight. Serve with tortilla chips.